THE
TRUE ORIGIN OF IGBO
AND HER CULTURE

IKEOKWU UGOCHUKWU BENJAMIN

Copyright © 2016 Ikeokwu Ugochukwu Benjamin

All rights reserved.

ISBN-13: 978-1539817802

ISBN-10: 1539817806

DEDICATION

I am dedicating this book to our first parents Adam and Eve and my good father, late Dr. H. Ikeokwu Onyenyiriqnwu. They are the twines with which the climbing rope of this palm tree is made.
May their souls rest in perfect peace.
Iseeee!.

CONTENTS

Dedication
About the book
Acknowledgement
Foreword
Benefits from this book

CHAPTER 1 -----------------   14
1 Igbo origin and culture
2 Punishments for Evil Acts in Igbo Race

CHAPTER TWO ----------   19
What is tradition and custom?
Culture contact
Origin of idol worship in the World
The origin of masquerade cult in Igbo tradition
Spiritual tradition
How the Igbo people greet
Igbo problems
Igbo language
Good Igbo nutritional value system/Odinala
Meaning of new yam
Good Igbo dressing system
Good Igbo tradition about death
Good Igbo tradition on giving birth to a child
A good Igbo child
Age grade

CHAPER THREE ----------   36
Good traditions on marriage
Payment of dowry and traditional marriage
The bride mother's money
Disagreement between a husband and the wife

CHAPTER FOUR ----------   43
Requisite knowledge before going into marriage
What those intending to marry should know

Secret thing in marriage
First thing in marriage
Fake marriage
The responsibility of the fathers in the family
Who is a man?
One thing every woman should know
Deep things in marriage
Responsibilities of a mother in the family

CHAPTER FIVE ------------------ **54**
Things that defile a man
Things that defile a woman
Uncleanliness and taboo
Some taboo to a woman
Taboo to the man
Taboo in Igbo land
Difference between taboo, defilement and sin
What defilement means
What taboo means
Suicide
Ameliorating the taboo to cleanse the land/Ikpualu

CHAPTER SIX --------------------- **60**
Breaking of kola nut
Leaving one's Father's compound to live elsewhere
Respect for the elders
Good elder and the ancestors
Bad elder

CHAPTER SEVEN ---------------- **65**
Ozo title-taking
Nze title holders
Elders titles/Ichie
Elders title cap
Coronation of a king and what itmeans/Igwe
Roles of a king Igwe and what his title stands for

CHAPTER EIGHT ------------- 72
God is with the Igbos forever
Elements of disintegration in Igbo land

CHAPTER NINE ---------------- 75
Second in command (Onowu)
Deputy to the king/Okpala, or Obi

CHAPTER TEN ----------------- 76
The meaning of Umuada and Umuokpu
The work of Ada/Umuokpu
What is Alumalu

CHAPTER ELEVEN ----------- 78
Igbo culture/ejirimara Igbo
What Igbos are supposed to learn
Where the Igbos are going
What is clearing the land?
What will the Igbos do?
The mystery
Those who scatter Igbos and the enemies of Igbos
How they are known
Religious practice
Good way of worshiping God

CHAPTER TWELVE ------------ 84
Singing
Benefits from singing songs
Dancing
Igbo and their mode of dressing
Types of clothes that the Igbos are supposed to wear
The types of food that the Igbos eat
Why the Igbos don't eat certain animals
What obtains in our land/Odinala
What obtains in a family (Odinaobi)
The good side
Bad side
What are we going to do in this situation/Odinaobu

CHAPTER THIRTEEN --------------- 95
What is a curse?
Different forms of curses
Things gotten from provoking God
Questions and answers on curse
What is outcast Or Osu?
Taking an oath
Questions and answers on oath
Reincarnation
Work of the devil
Can a dead person come out again?

CHAPTER FOURTEEN --------------- 102
What is Ofo?
How to produce staff of authority (ofo)
Giving somebody a staff of authority/ofo
How to establish a shrine/alusi
What power is in the shrine/alusi?
How Igbo prays in the olden days
How some Igbos value alligator pepper
What is an oath tree?

CHAPTER 15 ------------------------------- 109
When one is under the influence of a spirit (Agwu)
What does woman queen mean (Ezenwanyi)
What we should know
The work of a native doctor/Dibia
Omu (tender palm front)
Palm front (igunkwu)

CHAPTER 16 ------------------------------- 113
Destiny/Akara aka
Different types of gift
Other things you suppose to know
The best way to seek for our destiny

CHAPTER 17 ------------------------------- 115
Wines in Igbo land
Good wine tapper

Bad wine tapper
Ogwuduana wine
Wine intoxicated palm tree
What is ngwo?
How ngwo is tapped
A good ngwo wine tapper
A bad ngwo wine tapper
How to serve wine in the public
Wine for an occasion

CHAPTER 18 ------------------------ **121**
Making a will before one dies
Inheriting the wealth of a dead person
What is funeral ceremony/ikwaozu
Consequences of not burying a person
Good Burial and a bad type
Corpse of a full-fledged man
Corpse of a full-fledged woman
Burial with a bad taste
Slaughtering cow for somebody
Killing an animal for burial
Four market days in Igbo land

CHAPTER 19 ------------------------ **129**
Knowing and touching the word of God
Not having patience

CHAPTER 20 ------------------------ **131**
Advice to the youth
Advice to the church
Those that believe in devil
Biography

ACKNOWLEDGMENTS

This research, findings and writing was made possible with the help and assistance of a number of people. I therefore owe a lot to my mother Mrs. Alice M Onyenyirionwu, Professor Pita Ejiofor for the wonderful foreword writing. No words can adequately convey my gratitude to Barrister S.U. Anyia, Barrister Nwana Ifeoma E.S.Q, Rev. Fr. Patrick Chimezie OKeke, and Rev. Fr. Andrew Nwakelu, and Sr. B. Oguejiofor for patiently reading through the manuscript and making correction and constructive criticisms. Special thanks to Rev.Fr. Julian Anaeto, Rev. Fr. Paschalis. Agu and Rev. Fr. Hilary Ekwunibe for their encouragement. Many thanks to Mr. Jude Nwankwo for translating this work from Igbo to English and to all Bijec camera men. I am grateful to all who helped in typing the work- Miss Adah Ibeh, My gratitude goes to those authors whose literary works were made references to in this book, and to all Traditional rulers who helped me to achieve this goal. I owe an enormous debt to my lovely wife Mrs. Elizabeth C. Ikeokwu, my children Chisom J, Ekene G, Chukwuemezikam V. Ugochukwu for creating an enabling environment for this research. Above all, I give all the gory to my master, my Lord, our King and Lord Jesus Christ who lead me all through the research, writing and production of this book.

FOREWORD

I sincerely thank Mr. Ugochukwu Benjamin Ikeokwu on whom God bestowed special gift of deep thought that led to the research and findings that took him many years which has resulted in this work titled "THE TRUE ORIGIN OF IGBO AND HER CULTURE "
Every nation on earth has her origin as well as her tradition and what she avoids. In this book, Ugochukwu Ikeokwu is firm and resolute in his findings and postulations about the origin of the Igbos. He shows that Igbos are Jews by origin. He has his proofs of this.He also named the different Igbo traditions and from where they came. He further differentiated between the good traditions and bad ones.

The greatest of all is that he explained that God brought us the gospel in Igbo land to fulfill His promise to the Jews that he would be with them all the time and wherever they are. This book beckons on all Igbos to imbibe this gospel so that what God promised us will come to fulfillment.

In actual fact, a good product sells itself. My fellow Igbo compatriots, what the husband denied his wife has become very cheap in the market. I am so happy that at a time like this when tempest has been tossing a lot of Igbos around to the extent that many have lost focus, we still have a person like Ben who still has passion for the plight of the Igbos by creating time for the research involved in this book. Thanks to God that Igbos can still boast of a resourceful and passionate man.

This book outlines all that is Igbo tradition.
This simply means that every Igbo son will have this as a handbook, have it at home for teaching his children about Igbo tradition so that as soon as we retire, our children will not be left in the dark as to the right tradition of their fathers, rather, they will totally imbibe and continue the practice.

This book is supposed to be used in our schools as well as in the church since the church is about our traditions and our traditions are the church. This implies that since we are also God's chosen race, we must know God's will all the time and be able to know what He wants us to do at all time.

Finally, I plead with all Igbo people to get a copy of this book and put the contents to work knowing very well that if the bird 'ugo' throws away what it uses to beautify itself, its beauty is gone. Again, you don't tell a non-conformist that the war has broken out. Furthermore, an insect carried by 'Okpoko the bird is deaf. When one disregards his raffia calabash 'oba', the enemy will use it to collect and dispose ashes. It is the wood found in a clan that is used in cooking their food. Anyone who does not know where the rain started beating him or her, will not know where it stopped.

I salute anyone who will get this book for the purpose of promoting our culture and tradition.

Professor Pita Ejiofor
AWKA:MAY 2016
Founder 'Otu Suwakwa Igbo(Nigeria) INITIATIVE'
Former Vice-Chancellor, Nnamdi Azikiwe University, Awka

BENEFITS FROM THIS BOOK

The world is filled with confusion and lack of direction. This accounts for the confusion and division which is among the Igbos today. Concerning which way is the best to take where we are from and where we are heading to. Many of the Igbos are claiming that they are Christians but have no repentance. They simply pay lip service to going to church in order not to be categorized as sinners. In the same manner, many claim to be traditionalists but unfortunately, they don't even know what the tradition entails. They don't also know who the Igbos are and where they come from. They are just doing certain things because their forefathers did them but they do not know why their forefathers did what they did. Because of these, it is very important that anybody who is of Igbo origin should read and assimilate this book despite your level of education. It is also advisable that this book should be introduced in our schools so that this book will be used to teach pupils from primary to tertiary levels. Every family is supposed to have this book in their homes. Each son from Igbo land is also supposed to read this book for his or her own good and for the good of us all.

Many children of Igbo origin have gone through Primary, Secondary and University education but do not know what Igbo culture is all about or where come from Igbos. Even our language is hated with passion by them.

Let both our notable government officials, the leaders in the church and the head in schools circulate this book so that everybody, every family will have and know the content of this book and to put it into practice. This will definitely help us and enable our race to have a renewal of life and understanding.

CHAPTER ONE
IGBO ORIGIN

Before going to explain our tradition and culture, it is important to explain what Igbo is and its origin. The name "IGBO" is from a Hebrew name, whereas Hebrew itself is from somebody's name. That man is the great grandfather of Abraham referred to as "EBER" in the Bible. Igbos are Jew Hebrews. According to M.C.M IDIGO (1955) "One school of thought traces the origin of the Igbos from the Jews who migrated from Egypt centuries ago". V.M.C. Eyisi (2010) "The origin of the Igbos is traced as follows- from Adam-Noah-Shem-Eber-Abram-Jacob (Israel)-Gad-Eri (Gen.11; 10-26, Gen. 35; 23-26)". The first place the first group settled in Nigeria is Ubulu which is in Ebonyi state. According to Chisom Ani (2004) "The Igbos first settled in Calabar and in Ubulu because of the discovering of salt in Calabar and Ubulu, and Ubulu attracted a lot of them because of the availability of more natural resources" The next group set their foot at Aguleri which is today in Anambra state of Nigeria. M.C.M IDIGO (1955) Posited that "Eri with his followers landed and settled near the bank of the river Anambra called Omabala by the indigenes and corruptly named Anambra by the European settlers" Recent findings show that they came in three groups. The first group came in 718 BC, the second group came in 536 BC when Nebuchadnezzar won the Israelites at war. The third group landed in 70 AD when Titus divided Jerusalem. They came from different lineages like Gad lineage, Judia, Zebulom etc. They came through North Africa i.e. (Egypt, Morocco, Sudan, Ethiopia etc.) and came to Calabar. Through Calabar, they came to this place called Ubulu today. Ubulu was rich in salt and other resources. This made them to settle there. The original name they gave to this settlement was Hebrew. Because of difficulty in pronunciation and tongue configurations, the word "Ubulu' became a corruption of the word "Hebrew'. From "Ubulu" the pronunciation transformed to "Heebu", from "Heebu" to "Eboe", from "Eboe" to "Ibo" and finally to "Igbo". According to CVC (2012) "The Igbos are descendants of Jacob whose father was Abraham".

You can call them" Umuaro' or "Umu Eri" or "Umu Igbo". Whichever nomenclature they go by, what is important here is that they are Israelites-Hebrew (Ndi Juu). They are found in Abia, Akwa Ibom, Anambra, Cross River, Ebonyi, Edo, Enugu, Imo, Delta, Bayelsa, Benue, and Rivers State. To support these facts, the findings of one Mr. Olauda Equano from Isseke in Anambra state; a man sold into slavery into West Indies in the year 1789, found out that Igbo people and Jewish people have the same traditions. A white man, Dr. Basden an English missionary also gave a similar testimony in the year 1861.

There are myriads of testimonies that Igbo race originated from Israel. The Israelites themselves have come to Igbo land themselves and conducted a lot of research and findings whose video tape we have as a proof; which have also been aired in T.V. programmes that show the characteristics and traditions of Igbo people, which include Sacrifices, Festivals, Naming ceremonies, Marriage ceremonies etc. Giving somebody a name is significant in Igbo culture and it contrasts seriously with other cultures where a name is simply for identification. This explains why they give names like forest, road, cup, tree etc. to their children. According to Evang. C. A. Emmanuel (2008) "We are for now narrowing down our findings on the true origin of the Igbo race. The word of letters translated IGBO came from the name HEBREW". Igbos and Jews in the names they give to human beings reflect the belief that whatever name given to somebody follows that person and that the God that goes with the name creates. For more details about the Igbos, being the lost tribe of the Jews please I enjoin you to read the following books.

(a) **Complete information on Biafra by Chisom Ani (2004)**

(b) **The quest for the origin of the Igbo People by Uche P. Ikeanyibe.**

(c) **The Igbos as Descendants of Jacob by Eric C.N. Okam.**

(d) **The Igbo/Yoruba Politics by Anene Obianyido.**

And some video live interview of the following.
(a) H.R.H Eze C.N. Idigo 2nd of Aguleri.
(b) H.R.H. Igwe Emma Nnabuife of Isseke.
(c) H.R.H. Eze Obidiegwu Onyesoh of Nri.
(d) Barr J.J. Emeka of Enugu Aguleri.
(e) H.R.H. Eze Chukwuemeka Eri. Ezeora of Aguleri. With many certificate of recognition from the Israelites.

Punishment For Evil Acts In Igbo Race

Some acts are considered evil among the Igbos and Jews all over the world. Such acts include
a. Pre-marital Sex or Fornication
b. Homosexuality and Lesbianism
c. Bestiality or Zoophilia or sex between human and lesser animals
d. Pedophilia or sex with minors

Cultural Similarities Between Igbos and Jews
a. **Apprenticeship:** - This is a practice of serving a master for a number of years before being settled. It is common

phenomenon between the Igbos and their Jewish counterpart. It can last for five, six or seven years.

b. **Marriage:** The same cultural practice apply to both races. It involves meeting the parents of the bride and payment of dowry.

c. **Cleanliness:** It is a common practice in both races to brush and wash the mouth, wash the hands and the body and things bought from the market before eating them.

d. **Dances**: The people of these two cultures express their joy in functions and events through dances and singing of songs.

e. **Worship:** The two races worship God in every situation. No matter how bad a particular situation is, they must always remember their God.

f. **Development:** These two blood are very wonderful in development of wherever they find themselves. No wonder the whites say that' No Jew, no technology' as ninety percent of the world improvement could be ascribed to Jews so also development and change in Africa could be ascribed to the Igbos. No wonder Ifemesiani wrote concerning the lost Igbo/Jewish State in Africa "In Biafra Africa Died"

In 1997, some Israelites came to Igbo land to interpret what was written in the stone found in Aguleri. The stone was that of Gad written by our fore-fathers when they left Israel (ONYXSTONE) newly. As time passed, they forgot the language. When the invited Israelites came, they were able to interpret what was written on it and at "OBUGA/OBUGAD" built by Eri himself at Enugu Aguleri. Obu, or Obi is a house in the family wherein all members of the family meet to deliberate on common issues, and certain rules are made to protect its sacredness. V.M.C. Eyisi (2010) "He named the house 'obi Gad' (Gad's house) in honor of his father, Gad. He dedicated the house to God". It is the place where Ofo, Ikenga and other historic items are preserved; it is also a place where the oldest man in the family stays. In this obuga at aguleri, you will see David star drown at the wall of the building even at cloths and this David star is in our old Nigerian coin. The Israelites themselves already have the knowledge and the fact of our oneness and brotherhood with them. This explains the fact that they were the first to come to help us in the Nigerian/Biafra war in 1967. At that time, however, things were not very clear as for which step to take. The intention and direction were clearer during the leadership of President Ibrahim Badamusi Babangida. During this period, the Israelites came with a form requiring the intending returnee Igbos to fill. But Nigeria's leadership then did not support this and this put a stop to that agenda till today. In a portion of a video interview with Dr. Dozie Ikedife, whose hospital at Nnewi was one of the places the form was filled, he testified that about eight thousand candidates participated which I was one of them.

In the DNA test conducted by the Americans, and the ones conducted by the Israelites it was found out that the blood of the Igbos and that of the Jews are the same.
From the origin of the Igbos, we had to learning about the culture which changes from time to time. However, there are some development in culture and traditions that do not change. Culture and tradition that change so soon are: language, food, clothes, Behavioral patterns etc.

CHAPTER TWO
IGBO TRADITION AND CUSTOMS
What is Tradition and Custom?

The explanation already given about some Igbo traditions and the ones to be given now will help you to know what Igbo tradition is. 'Tradition' is the agreement between people living together as a town, village, kindred, different towns with common understanding (oha obodo etc.) It involves all they do to live in peace and harmony and with which they protect themselves. Tradition is handed from generation to generation; from parents to children to children's children, and such guidelines are known as norms. Some Igbo traditions 'omenala' to be explained are thus:

Ikwe ekele – Greetings

Iwa oji -Breaking of kola nut

Ipu obi -Leaving one's father's compound to go and build a house elsewhere to live in.

Isopuru okenye -Respecting the elders

Igba Egwu — -Dancing
Ichi ozo — -Ozo title-taking
Otu ogbo — -Age grade
Iri Ji — -(New) Yam festival
Ada/Okpu — -Daughters of the soil married to other places.
Alumalu — -Taking and giving in marriage

CULTURE CONTACT

A particular culture can add to itself and as such improve its contents through contacts with other cultures that is 'Acculturation' . E.B. Tylor "1832-1917" These appropriation can only last as long as they are useful to the receiving culture but can be discarded as soon as they are no more useful. Malinowski "1944"

Since Igbos originated from Israel and since the Israelite's spiritual tradition is serving God, the Igbos imbibed worshiping God fully.

Shrine-worshipping/alusi and masquerade cult are foreign to Igbo culture. It is the Xenocentric orientation/attitude that has been carried out by the Igbos that anything foreign is regarded as a 'paragon'.

Killing of twins is also foreign to Igbo culture.

Throwing away dead ones with swollen stomach as well as leprosy are sicknesses by which the Jews can isolate one but swollen stomach can be caused by other things like kidney problem. Ralph Linton states that, "The culture of a society is the way of life of its members, the collection of ideas and habits which they learn, share and transmit from generation to generation".

Many of the Jewish/Igbo traditions are given to them by God. Some are given through Moses and are contained in the ten commandments. Many of us do not know the real meaning of Igbo tradition. Some have the erroneous belief that our tradition is limited to shrine/alusi worshiping and masquerade cult. But importantly, these two are not parts and parcel of Igbo culture but are foreign to our culture.

BAD IGBO CULTURE.
Origin of Shrine Worshiping In The World

At one time or another mortal man has worshiped everything on the face of the earth, including himself. He has also worshiped everything imaginable in the sky and beneath the surface of the earth. Primitive man feared all manifestations of power; he worshiped every natural phenomenon he could not comprehend. The observation of powerful natural forces, such as storms, floods, earthquakes, landslides, volcanoes, fire, heat, and cold, greatly impressed the expanding mind of man. The first object to be worshiped by evolving man was a stone. Today the Kateri people of southern India still worship stone, as do numerous tribes in northern India.

Worship of Plants and Trees
Plants were first feared and then worshiped because of the intoxicating liquors which were derived from them. Primitive man believed that intoxication renders one divine. There was supposed to be something unusual and sacred about such an experience. Even in modern times alcohol is known as "spirits."
Early man looked upon sprouting grain with dread and superstitious awe so do some Igbos.

The Worship of Animals
Primitive man had a peculiar and fellow feeling for the higher animals. His ancestors had lived with them and even mated with them. In southern Asia it was earler believed that the souls of men came back to earth in animal form. In Igbo land, Some Igbos worshiped serpents/ekes, monkeys, snails, rabbits as their gods and ancestors. This belief was a survival of the still earlier practice of worshiping animals.

Worship of the Elements

Mankind has worshiped earth, like in Awlaw/Oro Oji river that worship the earth/ajana deity. Worship of air, water, and fire. The primitive races venerated springs and worshiped rivers. Even now in Mongolia and some part of Igbo land, there flourishes an influential river cult.

By the time of Noah nearly every person on earth was considered to be full of evil, even to the point that God himself "felt regrets that he made man on the earth, and he felt hurt at his heart."- Genesis 6:6. The earth had become so wicked and filled with corruption to the point that the earth needed to be wiped clean, just as an eraser to a slate/chalkboard. Later, a man by the name Nimrod (son of Cush, grandson of Ham, great-grandson of Noah) is the one who started post-deluvian idolatry. Nimrod (Hebrew: maradh'),meaning "rebel", was the founder and king of the first empire to come into existence after the Deluge. Nimrod's kingdom consisted of the cities of Babel, Erech, Accad and Calneh in the land of Shinar. Nimrod himself deified himself as a god above mankind". Why, then, was he called Nimrod? Because he stirred up the whole world to rebel (himrid) against his [God's]sovereignty."- Encyclopedia of Biblical Interpretation, by Menahem M. Kasher, Vol. II, 1955, p.79.Under the direction of Nimrod, the building of the tower of Babel began. Josephus wrote: "Nimrod little by little transformed the state of affairs into a tyranny holding that the only way to detach men from the fear of God was by making them continuously dependent upon his own power. He threatened to have his revenge on God. He wished to inundate the earth again; for he would build a tower higher than the water could reach and avenge the destruction of their forefathers. The people were eager to follow this advice of Nimrod, deeming it slavery to submit *to* God; so they set out to build the tower...and it rose with a speed beyond all expectations."-Jewish Antiquities, I, 114,115 (iv, 2, 3).

As the story went, God was angry with Nimrod for the dishonor he brought him and the false worship to himself he was demanding of the people,

so God frustrated the plans to complete the tower by confusing their language. In fact the word Babel means "confusion." The scattered people then went throughout the earth and settled in various locations,

taking with them not only their new language but also the false religious beliefs and idolatry learned from Nimrod, with them till date.

The origin of Masquerade Cult in Igbo Tradition.

The Igbo masquerades, mmanwu, are traditional performances acted out by exclusive secret societies within a community. These exclusive societies consist of adult male members, or some elderly women called Nne-mmanwu. Each member must be initiated into the society around the age of 14. Their identity is known only to the other members. The main function of these societies is to celebrate the harvest, "Ikwa ozu" - celebrating the dead, and to entertain the village people. Some other functions include enforcing village curfews, protection, and serving as village security guards. The members, also known as masqueraders, wear masks to hide their identity from the rest of the village. The mask is also worn to symbolize mermaid, coffin, animals and the spirit of a dead community member. By wearing the mask, a masquerader is thought to have spiritual powers that are conducted through the mask.

The living-dead are what these masquerade/spirits embody.

The beauty of dead "Mma-onwu". Igbo people believe that the dead never actually die; rather, they remain in a "personal immortal state". They reside somewhere between the earthly world and the spiritual world. These living-dead are believed to be closely related to those of the village. Since men are masqueraders, they are buried within their homes so their spirits may be close to their families. The living-dead then return to the earthly world from time to time to offer spiritual advice. It is the living-dead, who the masquerade portrays and the source of their powers is from the shrine/alusi.

In Igbo land, e.g. in Awlaw/Oro town of Oji-river L.G.A. There are visible masquerades meant for the public, such as, Uraga, Mgbadike, Ijere, Okwonma, Agabu, Agaba etc. They often are more entertaining. Masks used offer a visual appeal for their shapes and forms from the deity. In these visible masquerades, performances of harassment, music, dance, Ikonsi/charms, and some take human life each time their parodies are acted out. Some uses' human head, some animals in their sacrifices. Things Fall Apart by Chinua Achebe, F. Chidozie Ogbalu & E Nolue Emenanjo, Onwuejeogwu, "1975", Isichei, Elizabeth Allo (1997). A History of African Societies to "1870", Cambridge University Press, Olaudah Equiano, The Interesting Narrative of the Life of Olaudah Equiano, or Gustavus Vassa, the Africa.

The invisible masquerades take place at night. They include Achikwu, Ogbagu, Omenikoro. Sound is the main tool.

Main article: Mmanwu

Masquerade cult was introduced to Igbo society from Igala through the various intermarriages of Igbos with Igala people. The name of the first masquerade in Igbo land is called "ADAMEV or ADAMEFU", which started in the year (1212 AD), you can see all the pictures in our video. Many Igbos fancied it at first because of the work of policing (security) it was doing. Others adopted it for the purpose of recovering debts etc. Because of this, some masquerades still speak Igala in Igbo land today. Masquerading is a cultic activity of which every member that enters into it are possessed with evil spirit, and needs deliverance before one is free.

GOOD IGBO TRADITIONS
Spiritual Tradition

The foremost tradition of Igbo race is prayer and obedient to the almighty God. Deuteronomy 5;6 The Lord said, 'I am the Lord your God, who rescued you from Egypt, where you were slaves'. Worship no god but me. Do not bow down to any idol or worship it, for I am the LORD your God and I tolerate no rivals'. John 1; 17, 'God gave the law through Moses, but grace and truth came through Jesus Christ. 3; 36 'Whoever believes in the Son has eternal life; whoever disobeys the Son will not have life, but will remain under Gods punishment'. As St. Paul say;" There is one Lord, one faith(I.e. one true religion) one baptism" (Eph. Iv. 5) Despite the fact that Igbo crossed the Red sea and other countries of the world to come to the Eastern part of Nigeria, God did not forget them. As such, He blessed them with the word of God and prayer with which He fulfilled His promise to them. Our duty today as Igbos is to embrace the word of God and forget other foreign gods and adopt the good Igbo tradition which is now the light of the living God through Christ Jesus. Jeremiah 4; 1, The LORD says, "People of Israel/Igbo, if you want to turn, then turn back to me. If you are faithful to me and remove the idols I hate, it will be right for you to swear by my name. Then all the nations will ask me to bless them, and they will praise me".

How Igbo People Greet

Igbo people exchange greetings in a special and elaborate way. If an Igbo person sees you in the morning, he will greet you (ututu oma, Ibola chi, Isala chi) meaning "Good morning" He doesn't stop at this, he will ask you about your family in the following ways; "How is your family", "your parents"
They greet (Ehihie oma) in the afternoon "Good afternoon", in the evening they greet this way (Anyasi oma, Uhuruchi oma) "Good night" at night"(Kachiboo, Rahu juu, Kachifoo) May the day break" at night. When one is travelling we say (Gaagboo, Jee nke oma, Ije oma, Ejealo) "Safe journey". He "thanks you" when he received a favour from you in this way (Imeela, Imego, Anwula, Igaadi). "You will live long" when he has also received a favour. "Has your day brightened" in the morning, (Isaalachi, Iboolachi, Ibokwara) etc. Igbo people shake hands for those who are titled. For those titled ones, this is done thrice to show the four market days and must use the right hand. Igbos use the four market days in counting a week. When he is doing this, he expects you to tell him your praise name like "killer of lion' (Ogbuagu) "A powerful man of the Igbos" (Dike Igbo) "A Lion in a distant place"(Agumba) This is to show how close you are to his

heart. Other ways of greeting is by embracing; we do not greet by kissing or by bending down and touch the ground with our head or by prostrating on the ground as the Yorubas do in greeting. A full man in Igbo land does not have a handshake with a woman in Igbo land; rather he will rub his hand at her back. Likewise, in a handshake between an elder and a boy, it is the elder that will first of all thrust his hand out in invitation for handshake and not the young man. The Igbos wear a cheerful face in greeting as well as nodding of head. The Igbos express their joy in the public by stamping their feet on the ground in a public with a thunderous ovation and appraisal as well as dancing in a public. The Igbos also expresses respect to the elders by a child vacating a seat for an elder with greeting. Helping an elder out in carrying his load for him to his destination is a way of respect.

1. Igbo Problems:

The problem and the sickness of many of the Igbo people is that they do not know their language, where they come from and where they are going. They are like a large group of mad people in the market place, who neither know what they have come to buy nor when the market dismissed. There is total confusion among the Igbos today to the extent that crying is very difficult to them. According to Chikwelu Anietoo-Chukwu E. (2008) "Of a truth, Igbo people at present lack knowledge of what to do to solve their numerous political and spiritual problems, and also to understand what is the cause of these enormous confronting problems facing them". They are like that vegetable plant 'akidi' which does not know the land boundary. They are also people who are in a meeting who do not know what contributions to make. They are those who learn and outwits the person who taught them yet they don't know their own. They are the I too know but don't know his own. They behave like termites/akunkpu that have seen light and rejoice that it has seen something very wonderful that even if there is death there, they don't care to know. Those people called "Ndi Igbo" behave like dogs. The dog behaves this way: if you put yam for it, it will eat it, if you put cocoyam, it will abandon the yam and go to eat cocoyam. If you put tapioca at the same time, it will abandon the cocoyam for the tapioca. The same applies when you put meat or bones for it. Jeremiah 5; 26, "Evil men live among my people; they lie in wait like men who spread nets to catch birds, but they have set their traps to catch men. Just as a hunter fills his cage with loot. That is why they are powerful and rich, why they are fat and well fed. There is no limit to their evil deeds. They do not give orphans their rights or show justice to the oppressed. "But I the LORD, will punish them for these things; I will take revenge on this nation". Prophets speak nothing but lies;

Igbo Language

Igbo has a very nice language which is spiced by a lot of proverbs. Language is the life of a nation or any lineage. Once your language is removed from you, you look like a grasshopper whose wings has been clipped. This means that the person's power is gone. According to the Editorial of Bigard Theological Studies (2005) "Igbo identity is therefore identifiable through lasting Igbo cultural traits communicated through Igbo language".

You are to start teaching in Igbo language to any child you give birth to because he/she ought to speak in Igbo the first speech he will make. This is the language he is supposed to use to learn how to talk. Pita Ejiofor (2006) It is this same Igbo language that would serve as a communication language between you, your brothers and fellow Igbo brothers and sisters. One's sickness is very complicated if it is not identified. Now that we have identified our problems, our problems are over.

Good Igbo Nutritional Value system/Odinala

It is advised that Igbos should concentrate on eating those food found in their environment because God has given their land command about this. God has decreed that He would give us what to eat from the land' Odinala'. Eating too much of foreign food or eating only them has brought about a lot of untimely death to our fellow Igbo brothers and sisters.

Meaning of New Yam

The Igbos is one of the largest ethnic groups in Africa. In rural Nigeria, Igbo people work mostly as craftsmen, farmers and traders; they see yam as the highest crop just as kola nut is seen as the highest fruit. Yam is an important crop/plant that is the reason for proper preparation for farming (planting) yam i.e. clearing the farm, planting of yam seedling; it is the head of the family that will harvest the yam when it is due. It is the duty of the Igwe, or Obi/Qpara to tell his subjects that the yam is due for harvest. When the king declares that the yam is fit to eat, in the presence of his subjects; he dips yam into oil and eats to show the community that the yam is fit for eating, after this the people can now eat their yam and thank God. It does not mean that if somebody eats this yam in his house before igwe does so that he is going to die or something bad will happen to him but it is a sign of respect. It is the culture of the Igbos to show respect to the king and to the yam. The new yam festival is a big ceremony in Igbo land. People will be invited from neighbouring villages, towns, states and even neighbouring countries. All people will gather at the village square to appreciate God for the gift of new yam in that year and in other subsequent years. After which freewill donation will be made for the development of the community and handshakes will be exchanged.

There are different ways of eating yam, it could be roasted or cooked and eaten with oil or with breadfruit, it could be pounded and eaten with soup, any soup etc.

Good Igbo Dressing System

Many Igbos have abandoned our dressing code and borrowed bad foreign style. This is largely due to what they watch from films and home videos. Having known from this book that you are a special child of God, your dressing style must change. Why God gave Adam and Eve clothes in the Garden of Eden is to cover their nakedness and not to show it. This is as a result of their sin which caused them to be ashamed. In our society today, many people are no more ashamed; they wear seductive dresses, walk about naked and are not afraid of God anymore.

Good Igbo Tradition about Death

Igbos do this very well despite the fact that some overdo it. God created us in His image. As such, human body ought to be dignified even at death. As soon as one dies, his/her body is washed and is dressed in a good clothe. He/she is put in a coffin and is buried. He/she is paid the last respect through prayers. Those people related to him or her should be notified that the person is dead. Funeral activities are not supposed to be more than two or three days. Gomez, Michael Angelo(1998).For a young boy or girl, it is normally only a day. For one who has in-laws and grandchildren, it is up to two or three days. If it exceeds three days, know that the person is looking for something else. Funeral ceremony of a worthy man or woman in Igbo land is not done on the market day of the town of the deceased. This is because that day is the day the people go to buy and sell to get what they eat. But the deceased families can choose any day that is convenient to them it is not a taboo. In Igbo culture and tradition, there is nothing like free born, dedicated to idol/Osu or slave/Ohu. To designate and call another person such name is inhuman and a taboo. This shows that they do not have the fear of God. The people or a town like this should be enlightened by people who are knowledgeable and by the church too. During the funeral ceremonies of a full-fledged man or woman, cannon gun shots can be allowed or used but not for youths and women that is not up to 50 years. In scheduling a funeral ceremony, the family concerned can say that they want the ceremony to take place in a day only. This is worthy of emulation while some others may decide not to entertain any noise by disallowing any noise-causing activity.

GOOD IGBO TRADITION ON GIVING BIRTH TO A CHILD

Igbos do not do this in full today anymore. If a child is delivered in Igbo land, it is always a thing of joy. There is supposed to be joyous noise to show that a new child is born. If the child is a boy, he is to be circumcised, if a girl, she ought not to. There will be a ceremony of naming the child. This can go in pari-pasu with 'Omugwo' ceremony whereby the mother-in-law of the husband comes to take care of his wife and the child for a month or three months. Mostly, names such as Mgbeke (maiden born on the day of Eke), Mgborie (maiden born on the Orie day) Okeke, Nweke (male born on Eke day) Okafo, Nwafo (male born on Afo market day) were commonly our way of naming a child.

The naming ceremony is better done before the day of the churching ceremony of the child. The work of the parents of the child is to raise the child up in the fear and knowledge of the Lord and to teach him/her the language, tradition and culture of the Igbo race. If not the parents are offending the God that gave the child as well as the child himself and this brings about the child behaving like one who is a stranger "Mgbansi" in his own land. If a male child is born, the father will buy 3tubers of yam and 2 gallons of palm wine and smear the yam with traditional chalk (nzu) and take them to his in-laws. Once they see the smeared yam, they immediately know that the child is a male child. In the case of a female child, there is no smearing of the yam. At the in-laws place, the in-law will bring kola nut and break the kola nut after some pronouncements, and pray that God who brought the child will provide the means with which the child is to be taken care of. The father of the child and the mother in-law will then discuss about the visit of the mother in-law to the son-in-law to take care of the mother of the baby. This is called 'omugwo'. The mother of the new baby is taken care of very well in Igbo culture within this period. She is not allowed to do any difficult work between three weeks and a month and three weeks. A nursing mother during this period is quarantined. She does not move about anyhow or touch sacred things like a tuber of yam etc. If the navel of the child is done, it is buried in the soil. Some use the opportunity to give the new child a gift of cash crops like palm tree, bread fruit tree, pear tree by burying the navel of the child at the foot of the tree. This is known as 'Nkwana' in some dialect. Apart from this gift of tree, giving gift of different kinds to a new child is very common in Igbo land. People go to see a new child with gifts.

A GOOD IGBO CHILD

When an Igbo child wakes up in the morning, the first thing he does is to pray, dress his bed, go to greet his/her parents and members of his/her household. He/she then goes to wash his/her face, wash his mouth, sweeps the house and removes the over-night ash in the cooking place, warm the food and prepare for school.

A good Igbo child is holy because he respects every adult, he listens to his parents and teachers; he neither insults the teachers nor makes noise in the class. He does not cheat at work; he finishes his work before going to play. He does not tell lies nor come late for activities. He does not laugh at challenged persons and is always around his parents to learn stories and proverbs that will form and increase his wisdom and understanding. He is also ready to ask his parents and teachers questions about things that are unclear to him or her. As an individual person my child, you are a gift from God to yourself and to the family, community, and the entire Igbo nation. Always remember that you have these three values those meads you an Igbo person: The blood, the spirit, and the Igbo language. Daughters of St. Paul (1994) Out of his own love God decided to create you and give you a chance to exist. The gift of life is giving to you and God takes it back when he wills. God has freely given your life with its many gifts so that you too can share the gift of life to others. Your cultural background is a unique gift from God, which you need to esteem and appreciate by respecting your parents and elders. You are created in the image of God and his Spirit dwells in you. This indwelling Spirit needs to be nourished so that God's love may dwell in you. You can do this by developing a personal relationship with God through faith and by setting aside some time each day for prayers, reading the word of God in the Bible and reflection. Join and participate actively in religious movements in your church. As a young person you can improve your status in life by planning your resources well, such as the good use of your pocket money while at school or home, to buy e.g pencils, books, clothes. This will help you to manage the bigger resources which will be entrusted to your care in future. Be aware of who you are as a boy or girl. Keep yourself occupied. Avoid participating in destructive activities, idle talk, useless pat times, experimenting with your body, especially masturbation. Avoid pornography in all its forms. Avoid bad company. Develop healthy friendships with people of good character. Keep in touch with your parents. They always mean well for you and they are very willing to help you grow into a responsible person. Say an absolute "no" to sex outside marriage even if you are engaged. Avoid at all costs situations that can lead you into this temptation. Always communicate with your parents and seek their pieces of advice whenever need be. Never promise any person I will marry you or enter any covenant of blood in the name of I must marry you. Smoking is not good to your health, so avoid it. Do not believe in or worship another god except your God which is in heaven, the father of our Lord Jesus Christ. Remember that your parents and community at large will expect you to undertake responsibilities and will give them to you. Learn to accept responsibilities. You will be happy and much fulfilled when you find that you can handle what is assigned to you. When such is the case, your parents and superiors will be very proud of you and place a lot of trust in you.

Age Grade:

These are people born in the same year, or within one or two years. They start from their childhood to co-operate in every aspect of children's activities. They help each other until they come to the age of getting married. The roles of age grade are wide and encompassing, when it comes to development; it is the age grade that construct/repair the local bridges, churches, schools, bus tops, keeps security in villages, repair roads, sponsor brilliant children who have nobody to sponsor them, helping each other in time of marriage, death etc.

CHAPTER THREE
GOOD TRADITION ON MARRIAGE

In Igbo older tradition, an Igbo man or girl marries on recommendation and choice of the parents. Marriages were sometimes arranged from birth through negotiation of the two families. Men sometimes married multiple wives for economic reasons so as to have more people in the family, including children, to help on farms. Today however, the baton has changed. The man or the girl chooses for himself or herself whom to marry. This is as a result of culture contact with other cultures and culture influence there from and also as a result of advancement in education, human behaviour and technology and it is good. In this case, somebody can recommend you to somebody to marry but it is left for you to make a choice of that marriage. Rev. Fr. Dr. Innocent Ekumauche Okoh (1994) If a man sees his choice and both agree, the man will take one person (a man) and visit the parents of the girl she wants to marry. Rev. R.J. Griffin (where is the truth). He is expected to go with two pots of wine in this first attempt that denotes enquiry. These pots of wine are supposed to be shared and drank by both themselves and parents of the bride together with whoever the father of the girl wants to join in sharing the drinks with. It is in this first visit that the man makes his intention of marrying the girl known to the father. The father would receive their request and ask them to go and come back again during which he would ask the daughter about her intention over their request. They would ask her a lot of questions concerning the man. Such questions like: where did you know him , when did you know him?, what does he do?, His town, his friends?, residence, lineage, etc. It does not end here. Rev, Fr. Ezebuchi Paschalis Agu. (1996) They will go to enquire about the man and his lineage. In the same manner, the parents of the man will do the same thing for their son.

Other questions include whether there is theft in their blood; do they give poison?, do they die young?, or are they known for sudden death?, epilepsy?, witchcraft, Secret cult, are they involved in any taboo etc. Sonya Friedman (1983) When these necessary inquiries must have been made, the father of the girl to be married will invite people of his choice in the second visit, whereas the visitors i.e. the suitor will come with not more than three people with another two gallon of wine. If the enquiry is favourable, the father of the girl will invite his very close brothers; about two or three to come and witness what is going on. On that day, when two cups of wine must have gone round, the visitors will state what they come for. The father of the girl will now invite her to come before the visitors and she will be asked whether she has decided to marry the man. If she answers 'no' then there is a problem. In some cases, the father answers for the daughter in this case. If the visit is successful, a time will be fixed for visiting the land known as 'nleta ala' It is during this visit that the girl will go with the intending suitors people to the suitors place to see his place and remain there for a period of three weeks though nowadays people try to shorten the length of days involve. At the end of the visit, she will be clothed with a new dress and is given a pot of 'up wine' and accompanied with two girls from the suitors place to her home. One of the girls will hold the cup for drinking of the wine during the journey. John Powell (1981) As the journey progresses, when people see her, they will stop her and take a cup of wine from the pot and drink to show that they are happy in what is happening. If the wine finishes on the way, this shows that the people like the girl but if the girl is the type that does not greet people or lived a bad life, nobody will drink from her pot.

When she gets back to her father's house, she will tell her parents how she has gone to survey the place. If it is favourable, she will send back the pot, otherwise, the Suitors family will be asked to come and take back their pot. Where the going is good, at the returning of the pot, they will be told when to come to pay the dowry and take the girl. Before this, they must have been given the list of what are required.

PAYMENT OF DOWRY AND TRADITIONAL MARRIAGE

On the day of payment of dowry, the suitor's family will come with some elders; including the father. At the bride's family, a leading person will be selected. They will go into one room with some of the bride's parents and some selected few. After settling down, prayers and breaking of kola-nuts, and all the customaries observed, they will go to the customary rites of payment of dowry. It is to be noted that the wine for this purpose must be a traditional wine.

The bride's father will now demand for the witness who will now take the suitors outside for discussions/igbaizu. It is in this discussion that they will arrive at how much is to be given. But because there has to be some customary dowry in a plate for presentation. Herrada J. (1987) This is handed over to the lead person who hands it over to the father of the bride who in return hands it over to whoever he wants to count it for him who after counting says the amount to both parties. The father of the bride will say that it is not enough and they will go and discuss again. This process will continue until there is an agreement that will lead to the acceptance of the fee. If the bride's family does not want to waste time, the visitors will be asked to do it once or twice.

When the lead person hands over the money to the father of the bride, after counting, if he is satisfied, he will have a handshake with them and the daughter will be called and the father will hand over the plate containing the money to her and let her know that the money and the wine were brought for her in asking for her hands in marriage. If she accepts, she should return the money to him. If not, he would give them back the money. Eugene Kennedy, A. (1987) If the girl wants, she would kneel down, and hand over to the father the money and answer 'I have accepted' If so, the die is now cast, there would be clapping of hands.

A young man will rise to stamp his feet on the ground with enthusiasm and yelling of 'iyaaa!' from the people gathered. This is done whenever he stamps his foot on the ground. He does this severally. With this acceptance, the drinking of wine will increase.

Customarily speaking, any animal killed for this ceremony, the neck belongs to the leading person or witness.

THE BRIDE'S MOTHER'S MONEY

After the bride price had been paid, the mother of the bride is called in, the lead person is given a sum of money, that is half of the money the father received or lesser and she is told that this is the money with which she washed the napkins of the child and with which she also brought the child up. She will thank the people (in-laws) and pray for the success of the marriage. She will now leave to attend to other things.

The people that went for the dowry (The suitor) will now come out and give the different sets of people their customary dues. These groups are the father's 'Umunna' whose gifts are drinks, tobacco, potash, already grounded tobacco (snuff)eight or sixteen cola nut, yams etc.

Those of the women born in the bride's place but married to other places 'Umuada' will have their share which include drinks, salt, soap for washing clothes etc.

The boys of the bride kindred will have drinks, cigarettes etc. The girls that are not yet married will have drinks, soaps for bathing, chewing gum etc. Alualu inyomdi or inyomona will have there's too. However, all these provisions are not mandatory. Rev, Fr. Ezebuchi Paschalis Agu. (1996) The only mandatory thing is the bride price. As soon as the bride price is paid, the surname of the bride changes automatically to the suitor's surname. This is so automatic that even if at any instance she dies at that point, she will not be buried at her father's house but at her husband's house. At this instance too, the parents of the bride will also send her forth to her husband's house with gifts no matter how small. Even if it is not that day, it will be any other day. Engle woods Cliffs (1966) the last thing to be done for the bride is the blessing prayer of her father in her father's compound. It is note-worthy that this must necessarily be at her father's compound otherwise it is a taboo to have it done in another land or compound. When this prayer of blessing takes place, names of the ancestors that gave birth to the present generation of both the father of the suitor and the bride are called for assistance and blessings. This also signifies that the generation is continuous and will still continue.

The ceremony includes wine-giving by the father to the daughter to locate and give to her husband. This signifies a bond and serve also as a witness of handing over of the girl to the man she will hand over the wine to. This is done openly, and must be our local wine/nkwuenu.

The bride price vary from a girl to another mostly as a result of level of education. The bride price of a girl that went to university should not exceed N10, 000:00. Ten thousand naira. Most of the times when this bride price is paid for example for a graduate, the father of the bride may take only one thousand naira out of that and give the remaining back to the suitor and tell him that what is most important is for the two of them to live in peace. This shows that in Igbo tradition, a woman is not sold to the husband but just to fulfill the Igbo traditional ceremony. H.N. Wright (1982) At the same time, a wealthy man can build a house for his in-law which may cost him up to ten million naira whereas he only paid about six thousand naira as bride price. At the same time, if the father should count on how much he spent on the girl child, ten million naira may not be enough. The appeal and advice to all Igbos is that all towns, kindred should bring low the cost of marriage ceremonies in their places to enable young men and women engage in marriage.

DISAGREEMENT BETWEEN A HUSBAND AND THE WIFE

In a case of misunderstanding between the husband and the wife, it is always better for the two to reconcile. But when it becomes too difficult for them to reconcile by themselves, they are free to invite the third party of their choice to mediate between them. Okeke. H. O. (1993) but if the issue becomes so bad that the man does not want to marry the person again, he will send her home by using a pear leaf (akwukwo ube) to cover a pot of wine and take it to his in-law's house. Once it is done this way, it shows that the man does not want to live with the wife again. However, if he later decides to take her back again, he will provide wine, buy clothes for her and gather people to go to his in-law's house and plead to be given back his wife. Golden, M, (1981) But before this is done, he will first of all go alone to settle the scores between him and his wife to set the ground for smooth settlement. In a situation where the bride price has been returned because of quarrels and later the man still wants to marry the girl, in so far as the girl has not married another man, the former man can still marry her but this will take the shape of a new marriage. Blake Clark. (1970) In the same way, if it is the girl that decided to go on her own and later wants to go back, she can still go back but she will first of all mend fences with her husband by asking for forgiveness or even buy some gifts for him or do anything that will appeal to him.

CHAPTER FOUR
REQUISITE KNOWLEDGE BEFORE GOING INTO MARRIAGE

Every man and woman thinking of getting married supposed to know who is God before embarking on this life long journey. A woman is not supposed to have carnal knowledge or sexual intercourse with any man before getting married to a man. This is a taboo in Igbo culture. This attracts death since it is a law given by God to His people Israel and Igbos. Deuteronomy21;20- "But if the charge is true and there is no proof that the girl was a virgin, then they are to take her out to the entrance of her father's house where the men of her city are to stone her to death. She has done a shameful thing among our people by having intercourse before she was married, while she was still living in her father's house". Gillese, J. P. (1970) in the same manner, a man is not supposed to have a carnal knowledge of any other woman before marriage. All the pre-marital sexual relationship involved in by couples before marriage results in different problems that cannot be explained. The traditional medicine men (dibias) or mediums and false prophets cannot say this because they are not led by the spirit of God.

If a boy or a girl is having sexual urges, this is to show you that you are pathologically fit and that you are well made by God. John Paul 11, (1981) You will be cautious of not staying where you will be thinking about a lot of things like sexual relationship or nakedness. Watching pornographic films or reading pornographic books, seductive dances, seductive television programmes, seductive plays etc. This is also a reminder to those involving themselves that it is time to get married. One is supposed to tell their parents when they start having these desires rather than their friends. Mba C. S. (1986) having the desire of the opposite sex is neither a sin nor something evil or bad. What is evil however is ruminating idly on these thoughts when you know that it will lead you into what you are not yet prepared for. A married man or woman is not supposed to sleep with another person because this is tantamount to one defying himself or herself, which causes the failure or destruction of the home. A man and woman or a couple who have sexual relationship without defying themselves eventually have children who are heroes, wrestlers, outstanding men, renowned strong men. You can't impose any charms on them because they are as God created them. Mc. Sweeney, E. (1992) Murderers don't have any power over them, many sicknesses are not for them. Evil spirit run away from them. Wherever they go, outstanding things and wonderful things is said about them. People like that should not be misled into going for charms or secret cult for protection or progress since it will not work for that person because the power in such person is greater than the powers he goes about looking for.

WHAT THOSE INTENDING FOR MARRIAGE SHOULD KNOW

If a man has been involved in sexual relationship and the girl has not, they are supposed to tell each other the truth about themselves. Miller, D. F. (1974) whatever you hide from the person you intend to marry; you are sowing the seed of failure to your family. Mullally, M. V., (1972) Questions you are supposed to ask each other are as follow: how many boys or girls you have dated. How many times do you want sex in a week. How many children are we going to have. What engages the other person, what makes each other happy, the type of food each of them enjoy, what interests each other, whether any of them drinks alcohol or not, whether they take snuff or not. Telling each other the truth will make the family live in peace and united. Wright, H. N. (1982) If the foundation of the family is laid with lies, the family will likely collapse.

Secret things in marriage

If your wife is eighteen years old when you married her, it will take another eighteen years before both character become one. If you don't know all these things, thinking that your wife will be as you like in a twinkle of an eye, mind you that you are the problem. According to Rev. R. J. Griffin in a book where is the truth. Chapter 3 section 2, page 72. "Find out all you can about the girl you think you love even before letting her know that you want her".

First Thing in Marriage

You don't marry because you want to have a child, nor because your mate is getting married nor your parents needed grandchildren. This belief is what we have in Igbo land, it is very bad. The reason for marriage is for helping each other; it is a call. In addition to that we fail to do the will of God and it causes a lot of problem today. Man is not complete, so do woman. AECAWA, (1986) If your wife is pregnant, this is good, and you have a double blessing, and your responsibility is also double when Adam was created, it took so many years before Eve was brought to him.

When God created them, they lived in peace and in Joy for years before they committed the sin of eating the fruit God told them not to eat, it was then that delivering took place in the whole world, these shows that delivering is second blessing and it is not the topic for marriage.

The Igbos misunderstand this, thinking that anybody his wife has not delivered is a curse, that is not true. M.M.M. Drogheda, Ireland (1979) Believing that a child is the reason for getting married has caused a lot of problem and God is not happy with that. If your wife is pregnant, good and fine; from that day on, the training of that child she is pregnant of will start. Rev, Fr. Joseph Nwilo (2003) state that "The period of pregnancy is one of the deciding states in the formation of the baby". A man that marries should change some character traits he lived with before; he will stop too much drinking, smoking, wasting of time, much journey, staying outside till (six o' clock pm) etc. Daley, C. (1983) the kind of life you lived since you were born must change, and if you get your wife pregnant with that old character, it means that the message you sent will be brought back to you. When your wife is pregnant, you are supposed to be close to her always helping her in so many ways, because the love you are showing her is also touching the baby she is pregnant of. (Eph.5.20) There is no other work greater than taking care of your family, this is the will of God and it is the reason God called you to be a father; doing this entire thing you will see the kingdom of God. Igbo's there is nothing greater than being "HUSBAND and WIFE". It is the first ordination on this earth we are today, while other one's continue from it. (Gal. 3; 27-28) Another responsibility is to train your children. It is good for both of you to decide the number of children you will give birth to, this is very important. God gave every woman eight days in every month to take in, so you don't need to say that it is God who gives and trains children. There is every tendency in your family that is church and politics, so don't say the child is by surprise, stand in truth and also pray in the morning, afternoon and night, the God that called you for the work will help you so that you can train those children that he handed over to you. (Genesis 1; 27) Remember you are called for help, so don't take it as your own. Due to these reasons people make mistakes thinking that they are the owner of those children they born. Please teach your children the rules of God, the rules in the country, what to do and what not to do, what sin is, what taboo is, and also teach them what is good. Mrs. Norman Vincent (1971) when they are mature, teach them what is man and woman so that they will know the part to follow once they get to cross-roads or where they have four ways.

Show your children frog in a stone, you touch it, one, by practicalizing what you say not only by word of mouth. Remember, children are like a gun, once you release the trigger it will bounce on the nearby person. But if you keep a perfume the person close to it also will perceive the fragrance. If you teach them bad character, know it that you are the first to receive the blow. In the same way, a child who is continually derided by the parents as being stupid, hopeless etc. may eventually grow up with such image of himself indelibly printed in his mind as a portrait of his worth. If you show your son who is God, God will show them their parent. Dobson J. (1982).

FAKE MARRIAGE

The person you want to marry must know these things;
(a) Have you done any abortion before?
(b) Do you have any child or married before?
(c) Have you been in, or in any secret society?
(d) Are you in any covenant for marriage with anybody?
(e) Have you tampered with your womb before?
(f) Are you impotent?

(g) Did you have any mental illness before?
Hiding any of these things to the person you want to marry, you should know that your marriage is fake and not marriage in the first place.

THE RESPONSIBILITY OF THE FATHERS IN THE FAMILY

This work starts when the person is still a youth. Any male that grows in his father's house should know that to put his father's house-hood in order this is done by ensuring that his mother and father are being fed well; clothed and have their dues in the village or town paid, church dues. SCDF. dcr. May 13, (1977). He will make sure that the person to prepare the food for them when they are getting old is available. Born to love by Rev, Fr. Ezebuchi Paschalis Agu. (1996) the work includes washing clothes for them since they are too old for this. If there is no house in the compound, the person will provide this before going to erect a house to live in if he can afford this.

WHO IS A MAN

A man is neither somebody that is tall nor somebody that have hairs in the jaws. Harold R. Nelson (1966) As human person, you were formed from one relationship in order to grow into relationship with other human persons. God breathed into you the 'breath of life' and because of this you have the potential for goodness, the knowledge of good and evil. You are therefore able to develop values and intentions in life. A man must be somebody that have the mind to carry load, mind to represent his intellect, mind to think out something and also strong for work, he does not get tired to work, he always think about the family and how to make a happy home. J. Allan Petersen (1973) In Igbo community, you may donate 10m naira to them they will clap for you, but will always regard you as nothing but "Okoro" not until you have a family you are taking care of. That is when you are known as "Dibiuno or Diuhu". Keeping the wife and the children good disturbs him; somebody that can die for the family is a man. Gabriel John (1964) A man is that person that have gone through trials and temptations, but remain calm with his God. Being a man distinguishes you from all other creatures because you possess an eternal soul and your reasoning powers are high. This is a gift from God who wishes you to live with him eternally. Every man supposed to know who is God before he thinks of having a family. Any family that does not fear God is like the dog that is climbing an (Iroko tree). A man should know his father, his mother, everything about his family, kindred, history about his tribe and also his village, his culture and language. All these things make up a man. William E. (1964)

ONE THING EVERY WOMAN SHOULD KNOW

Any man that came to marry you loves you as if to say you are the highest among every other women on earth. A good wife should live with one mind with her husband, once you are the only woman he is married to, he looks after you, why do you have double mind about your husband?.

DEEP THINGS IN MARRIAGE

Love is not two, it does not come by chance; it is developed and it lasts till death. You cannot love two people at a time. This is the reason God want every man to marry-one wife till death do them part. 25th years of our research shows that some Igbos do not know what is love. God gave a command that every man should love his wife. Good character does not indicate love to the opposite person. According to Rev, Fr. Ezebuchi Paschalis Agu. (1996) "When you hear and see people say I love you, consider how emotion, passion, greed, lust, desire and self-satisfaction that are vented in their words" Any money a man gives to the person that is not his wife is invaluable except that you give in place of it help from which you receive the reward from heaven. (Mtt 19; 5-6) Women should also know that no matter the condition of your husband you will not let another man to sleep with you. Martha Nelson (1972) if another man should sleep with you outside your husband; it shows that you are a prostitute. Chukwuemeka Nweke stated that "Adultery is a grave sin, a sacrilege that brings about God's automatic withdrawal from a marriage" Husband and wife have no reason to say that one should not accept each other. This is a crime. Denying your husband or wife pleasure is a great sin before God. (Ex. 20;14) and (1 Cor. 6; 13) There is nothing like praying and fasting etc. that will make you deny your spouse some comfort. Leslie Parrott (1970) Rejecting your husband or your wife means you are separating what God have joined together. The only condition that justifies this is sickness.

Example: If this man loves his wife, he will not do anything with any other woman on earth than the one he did to his wife.(Mtt 19 ; 6)There is no other love he will show to any other woman than the one shown to his wife, except they agree in one mind to do for another woman and not for him alone. Eileen Guder (1965) but this does not mean after marriage that you pursue your mother and your siblings. You must show them love but mind you that you must know the size of your pocket. This is not the love of mouth (I love you) it is a story of tortoise, once you are deceived you are gone, all these are wickedness. After training your children, they will also continue to train you as their parents.

Responsibilities of a mother in the family

Who is a woman?

A woman is not the person that covers her hair, nor wearing earrings, not also somebody that rubs lipstick, eye shadow nor did manicure and pedicure or either wearing seductive or short dress. A woman is not some one that attempts to drastically change her natural bodily make-up.

A woman is God's creature that follows the good step of her parent's to grow and she knows she is a woman that she deserves respect. Eugenia Price (1962) a woman should know the word of God and boast with it. A woman respects the elders, says the truth, greets people anywhere, does the domestic work, learns to cook very well, and learns to keep the environment clean. You know a good woman when you see one by what she does; she keeps the environs clean without being told and everywhere will be looking beautiful. Any family that has a good woman/girl is always happy because you cannot remind her of any domestic work. But once she left the family the mother will continue the domestic work where she stopped before leaving the family. Gladys Hunt (1972) a good woman looks smart and attractive by being well-groomed, clean and well dressed. People admire her when she looks polite, pleasant and well-mannered. You are feminine, and you can improve your femininity by understanding your physical and emotional development and behaving accordingly. The good woman needs to know both and understand the changes that take place in her as she grows physically and to try to cope with them. In the Genesis story of creation, we read: "God said, 'Let us make man in our image, after our likeness'" In his image he made them male and female. All other creatures were talked into being but God used his "hands" to mold Adam and Eve: the first human persons. Grand Rapids, Mich (1970) This shows how special each one of us is and the dignity God has bestowed upon us.

Any woman that has shame, covers her body very well, this shows that she is mature enough. But any one that has no shame, the man that marries her should be pitied. A woman that stays close to her good mother picks a good history. She knows when it is time to add salt to the soup and not alone cooking. She learns the basic thing a good woman should know like housekeeping, cooking, and child care. She respects her parents until she gets married. Arlene Francis (1960) once she is married in a family she also helps that family because she does not separate the husband from his siblings. With the respect and humility she gives her husband joy, which makes her husband not to be outside till 6 o'clock pm. She accepts her husband and does not argue with him all the time. Once she gives birth to a child she looks after them very well. A woman stays with "love" and Patience in every condition of her husband, she always plead for forgiveness with her husband at all time. She teaches her children how to pray and not how to live a way-ward life but to be neat and with good character. Rev. R.J Griffin you need this book called where is the truth? Some men should know that a woman who left her family to his own family loves him very much more than every other man on earth. Men should have patient, humility and love towards their wife because they are not strong like them. Charlene Johnson (1961) Women should know that any respect to your husband is not given to any other man. Husband and wife after training your children, they will also train you too.

CHAPTER FIVE
THINGS THAT DEFILE A MAN

Things that defile a man are the following: worshiping other creature which is meant to serve man. Sleeping with a woman that is not one's wife, murder, false accusation, stealing, stealing by trick (419), owing, unworthy of trust, appropriating public wealth to oneself, sexual relationship with animals. These and other things are the things that defile a man and causes him unexplainable problems without solutions.

THINGS THAT DEFILE A WOMAN

Having sexual relationship with a man other than one's husband, or any sex during one's period, jealous, wearing clothes that exposes the body; seducing a man that is not one's husband. Trusting in created things other than God, dancing seductively in public, sexual relations with animals or spirit, stealing, belonging to witchcraft, marine kingdom etc.

Uncleanliness and Taboos

These apply to the following anomalies:

Ikwa Ikwo: Having sexual relationship with someone who is still underage.

Ikwa Inyo: Sexual interaction between a man and a man or a woman with a woman.

Igba Ikwo: Sexual relationship between a person and an animal. This type of uncleanliness is so serious that it goes from one generation to the other and results in total annihilation. God told our fore-fathers in the bible that whosoever indulges in these, his name will be struck off from the book of life.

Some Taboos to The Woman
Flirting, discussing the secrets of masquerade unless one is an elderly woman that is a matron to masquerade; touching kola presented to the public; eating 'eke-okuko'; touching a tuber of yam when she is still in her period, climbing a cola tree, palm tree; fighting in a market place, breaking kola-nut in the present of a man or a boy, woman giving a woman in marriage, collecting a bride price by herself, performing customary rituals with kola-nut, worshipping God with uncovered hair, holding the insignia of office (ofo) in her hands, having a bald shaving when not directed by her husband, abusing her husband's kindred or clan. A woman and her brothers cannot have sexual intimacy, they cannot marry until three generations pass. Talking to a man while crossing her legs; giving something to her senior with left hand; sitting carelessly, spreading or carelessly littering her cleaning pad anyhow; cutting an economic tree and a productive tree, going to determine land boundary, selling of family land etc.

Taboos to The man
Sleeping with another man's wife, removing a planted yam, stealing a planted yam, removing a planted beacon secretly, covering your head while praying when you are not a bishop. Sleeping with a woman in her period, insulting and abusing a gathering, giving poison, stealing, beating either of the parents in any way at all. Deceiving or fighting them from the back door, backbiting, removing a tree or plants planted by another person in his own land and not in yours. Laughing at one's father's or mother's nakedness, indulging in scams and frauds. Using or eating what somebody gives you to keep for him like money. Appropriating what

belongs to a group. Not keeping what you agreed to keep when you were given a title. Dressing like an anointed or titled men or priests (impersonation), ozo, king, ichie when one is not one of them. Cheating a widow or a child whose parents are dead, discussing acts, talks and even keeping silence when things are going wrong. Using left hand to give an elder something. Finally, sitting down when an elder is standing, or any other form of disrespect to an elder.

Taboos in Igbo Land

Taboos and things to be avoided are similar but taboos are weightier. These are taboos in Igbo tradition: murder, suicide, worshiping idols, selling human beings, cursing a group of people, sexual relationship between a person and an animal (IgbaIkwo); sexual relationship between people of the same sex; sleeping with one's mother, brother or sister or children. Using charm for love or for marriage, Killing a pregnant woman i.e. (a woman and the child); beating one's father or mother, or curses his father or his mother, this attracts death penalty. Giving out a girl with Child in marriage secretly, having a child out of wedlock, this child is a curse to you, kidnapping. Eating people's money, desecrating Holy things; willfully misleading a child, fighting and backbiting one's kindred, town or race. Castigating God or His anointed; killing one's spirit by false accusation and obtaining by trick known as (419); selling of human parts, stealing of human beings, making sacrifices to things, beings, or spirit created by God, worshiping anything except the Creator. Drinking of blood of any type except that of Jesus Christ. Leviticus 20;13 If a man has sexual relations with another man, they have done a disgusting thing, and both shall be put to death, etc.

Difference between taboo, Defilement and sin

Both taboos, defilement and sin are all evil but they are not the same.

Sin/Njo: A man that sleeps with a woman who is not his wife has committed sin because they are not husband and wife/Ikwaiko.

Defilement/NSo: When this woman sleeps with this man who is not her husband when she is in her period she has defiled the land, the man, and the bed used and has committed the sin of fornication, i.e. three in one act.

Explaining Taboo/ALU:

Any man that sleeps with another man's wife has committed a taboo/alu with that woman. The same thing applies to sleeping with a fellow man, animals, and little girls whether it is his own child or not. Using charms for love or for marriage is a taboo. Having a child out of wedlock, any kind of spilling human blood, worshiping or sacrificing to any god, or spirit other than the Creator etc.

Sin/njo: Sin is an evil but it is easier to forgive. This can be forgiven first by the person to whom that has been done to, then by God but there is always a punishment that goes with it even after the offence has been forgiven.

What defilement means/Nso

Defilement is staining what God has created. It is like one who is wearing white clothes which has red oil poured on it. This disgusts every person that sees it including the person that wears it. To atone for those defilements is very difficult. It is more than apologizing to the person that wears the cloth. This can lead to the destruction of that clothe. Whoever that defiles has defiled himself, the land, the house, the thing and the place where the defilement is done. It is only God that can remake the defiled to be Holy again, read Leviticus 1 to end.

What taboo means/Alu

A taboo "ALU" is a vehement prohibition of an action based on the belief that such behavior is either too sacred or too accursed for ordinary individuals to undertake, under threat of supernatural punishment. B. D. (1992)one who commits a taboo is like preparing for death. A taboo is not forgiven easily. Every taboo should be ameliorated (Ikpu alu). It is not forgiven so easily. Dixon, Robert M. W.(1988).Not even God forgives a taboo until He punishes whoever commits it. We read about David who slept with somebody's wife and after killed the husband of the woman so that the man would not know that he had impregnated the woman. Likewise Cain killed his brother Abel. Lewis, N. (1983). These have their long-lasting consequences. A lot of troubles in the world today, are as a result of a lot of taboos committed by people who think that there is another way they could circumvent the punishment associated with this taboo. Some of these taboos are: murder, disrespect to your Creator, frustrating your fellow human being thinking that you are educated or developed. Nobody would buy God over in this case; nor bribe God. Once committed, God and the land continue to go after and punish the person and no other power can save the person except God's power.

Suicide:
Suicide or killing oneself is a very serious taboo in Igbo land. Both the trees, home, rope, gun, knife and all the effects of the person involved are considered as

taboo as well as where the incidence happened.

What this means is that nobody has the right to terminate a life whether it is another person's life or his own life in any way at all. Harris, Lisa (2008). What this implies is that the wrong must be righted. The taboo must be ameliorated so that peace will be restored.

Ameliorating taboo to cleanse the land/IKPU ALU:

The only person that can ameliorate taboo to cleanse the land is God, through the behavior of the people of God. That is when they have committed taboo against the land and the human beings. It is God the creator who can now give the land order to be still. In actual fact, God created the world in what we are into twelve sections, eleven and half have pass before Jesus came. Lewis, N. (1983).When Jesus came, he came at the appointed and at the end of time to wipe out all the impunities and sins committed. It is as a result of this that He was crucified on the cross which is a way of killing those who committed atrocities. This is to show that the son of man that did not commit atrocity died on the cross of atrocity to nullify atrocity; for all of us who have committed taboos or atrocity and sin in the world. Therefore, whoever that is to nullify or ameliorate any taboo must get power from the power that is in the sacrifice Christ did at the cross. If not, it is not valid.

CHAPTER SIX
Breaking of Kola-nut

Igbos consider the kola seed as the greatest of all other seeds. Any family man whether titled or not is supposed to have kola at every point in time in his house. As such, they will offer you kola when you visit them. Every traditional ceremony starts with breaking and eating of kola-nut. It is through the breaking of kola-nut that Igbos prays and talk to God as well as the land and the forefathers. Breaking of kola-nut is done by a man. A woman cannot break kola-nut when the man is there; a child cannot do it when there is an elder. An ordinary man cannot break kola-nut where there is a titled man unless he is told to do so.

If the kola-nut is brought in the public it must be four, eight, twelve and nothing else is said until the kola is broken because the intention is to first of all talk to God through the kola and break it. C.V.C (2012) Opined that "Kola or kola-nut as it is commonly called is a fruit seed gotten or derived from a tree plant called kola tree". The Igbos say that once a kola is brought, long talks arise, because as the breaking of kola words go on, the kola itself is believed to embark on a journey after which it comes back when the breaking processes must have been concluded. What this shows is for example, if there is a ceremony at Okeke's house, when the ceremony is set Okeke's wife will bring the kola to Okeke to present to the people. Okeke will give his brother the kola to present to the people. If there is a person from their town Umudim, that came with the visitors, the kola will be given to him. He will now present the kola to the visitors. The kola will start from the nearest house to the farthest before returning to Okeke's house. If the kola are many, it will be given to the visitors from distant places so that the kola will get home before it is broken. At this juncture, the kola can be broken by Okeke or given to an elder from his side to be broken for him. Oguejiofor (1996) after breaking the kola, he will tell the people how many robes the kola has before he is called his praise names and the eating of the kola takes place. This is done with a kola of Igbo's specie. Hence, the kola can have up to three, four, five six or seven robes. Whatever the number of the robes has a significance in Igbo land. A kola with seven robes is a great one and merriment is supposed to be organized for it.

Leaving One's Father's Compound To Live Elsewhere/Ipu obi

Moving out of one's father's compound to make a home is done by Igbos when they have grown into manhood. A man who has three sons will share the land for them when he is still alive. Since the first son already inherits the father's compound by right and will get a farming land, which others will get if there is enough land. Any young man that is of age or has gotten money to build a house will be given a land to build a house. Every man given birth to must have a land to build in, even if the person is an imbecile.

If the father of the family did not divide his landed property, before he dies, it is the duty of the first son and his father's brothers to share their fathers land for the first son and his brothers. Fr. Rich. N. Ekegbo (2000) "But those who cannot train their children need not match to marriage or they would be paying the society with a double score of wretches". If the first son arrogates the whole land only to himself and leave the brothers out, this is defiling the land and this brings about the land being hot. Any sin committed against the land brings about the land being hot and it attracts problems to those living in it, or those farming on it or those harvesting the crops from it. Those anomalies that can cause this are: one gradually taking another person's land, or taking it by force or secretly because nobody knows about the land. If it is not as a result of the fact that the owner of the land has died, or as a result that the people do not know what is their father's. whichever way you take a land that does not belong to you, will bring about the land getting hot and its consequences. The land getting hot brings about untimely death, at times, it kills every newborn child in the family, despite the fact that he who stole the land had died long time before and the people alive do not know anything about it. To remove a plant that serves as a land demarcation or boundary brings about this hotness of the land too. The land getting hot can bring sickness, inability to progress, inability to marry, madness and sudden death. If the father did not divide the land before he dies, it is the duty of the first son to ensure that this is done, otherwise, he has put his children to suffer.

RESPECT FOR THE ELDERS

In the whole Igbo land, it is the elders that rule. All other nations of the world are ruled by presidents except Israel. It is the elders that organize things there. The same applies to the Igbos, which explains why the Igbos respect the elders so much. Mbaebie Joyce (2009) stated that "Each elder possessed domestic authority because he was the intermediary between the family and the ancestors" See also Meek, C.K. (1973). As such a child is supposed to vacate a seat for an elder in a gathering. "The bones of the elders cut like a knife" it is said. This implies that disrespect to an elder attracts blame, fall and drawback. At the same time, the elders must also be clean. An elder that sees where something is going wrong must speak against it; so that saying, "seeing but not saying results in the decaying of the elder's eyes when he dies whereas saying without hearing results in a sudden death for a child", will always hold.

The elders are highly regarded and respected in Igbo land. This is because it is the elders that mediate in the different problems in the land such as land cases, cases about cash crops, unjust treatment, a case between a town and another town, generational stories, marriage cases, stipulating how things should go and instructing the land etc. Elders are gifts from God because it does not come as a result of grey hair. The elders are also the ancestors. That is why the Igbos call on them because they were the owners of the land. The Igbos call on them whether they are still alive or dead. The elders are the people called when the 'Ichies' are called because the Igbos believe in resurrection. That's why they believe that these ancestors will answer them when things become difficult for them. The Igbos believe that death is about the abandonment of the flesh, whereas the soul has not died at all. It is to these ancestors that the people throw the heart of the kola-nut after the breaking of the kola-nut. The same applies to food and wine. Thus, he who offends the elder is under punishment. The elders referred to here are good elder because we have bad elders too.

Good Elders and The Ancestors

The good elder is one with integrity; if he has a family, he takes good care of the children and wife; he is always in thoughts all the time thinking about how to put food on the table for his family, school fees, how to protect them from the enemies, teaching them how to fear God and those things that defile the land. He does not involve himself in evil things. He contributes to the development of his town. He always says the truth whenever called upon to do this despite the problems associated with telling the truth. A good elder will always contribute whatever he can to ensure that there is peace in his family, town, etc. He does this through talks, meditations, contacts, counseling, good conduct and good dressing.

Bad Elder

A bad elder is known for giving poison, witchcraft, gossiping, drunkenness, and stealing, bad example, back-biting one ageist who wants to marry or to be married, over ambition, selfishness, troublemaking, and bribery. Taking another man's bait, bad counseling, silence where truth is to be said pregnanting women everywhere etc. An elder like this is not among the ancestors we talk about.

CHAPTER SEVEN
Ozo Title-Taking

Igbo people take ozo title to show that they are wealthy. This ceremony is a very big one because of the huge financial involvement it entails. It is for those persons who have money. If a man sees himself as a very rich man, he will approach the ozo titled members to indicate his interest in the title. Meek, C. (1937). They in return will examine the person to see if he is qualified before they agree to accept him in their fold. They will find out whether he got his riches in a good way or whether he is a good person; whether he breaks the laws of the land etc. If they found out that the person is qualified, they will now agree to accept him and give him the title. The person will now dole out money to meet all that is required of him according to the laws of the group. He will now cook assorted types of food to entertain the people with. Achebe, C. (1957). Things Fall Apart, Pub. London.

The work of 'Ozo' title holder in the land is to help in ensuring that there is peace in the land and development of the town. It is no longer a matter of neither shrine/Alusi nor evil spirit as done in the olden days. If the need for money comes up, the ozo people are called upon. Agbakoba, J., and Nwauche, E. (2006), They will come and live to their bidding. Ozo title taking is not an elder's affair as such because a child that is breast-feeding can still be made an ozo through the title taking of course in so far as the person to sponsor him is there.

Nze Title Holders

Nze title holders are those who are qualified by having good character and those who have done good things for the town. Arth. M. (1968). An nze title holder must be a full-fledged, thoughtful and good-mannered man. The full meaning of 'nze' is "Ndi Na-Ezere Njo" meaning "Those who avoid sin" Holiness is 'nze'. If for example Mr Okeke is known for good character, and has done for the town a lot of good things without pressure to do that. A person can also solve certain problems for a town and at the same time is known for goodness who does not over do things and is respected. Jeffreys, M. (1951). With all these, the people will bring out such people and beg him to receive the chieftaincy title Nze. If eventually, later the person turns to a bad life, he will be stripped of the title. The same applies to Ozo title. It is expected that any nze title holder must be financially independent person and capable person in all respects so that if a town is in need, the nze title holders can be called upon to help. Ogbukagu, I.K. (1997). "Traditional Igbo beliefs and Practices". Basden, G. (1921). " Among the Ibos of Nigeria" Pub Nonsuch, p.211-213

These titled men are to see that a town is well positioned for anything that can challenge them. V.M.C. Eyisi (2010) "Nze title is both a responsibility and honour awarded to a person by a community to represent and serve the community as a member of the Eze-in-council, while Ozo title is a prestigious traditional title taken by choice by man who can afford the expenses". There are other titles in Igbo land. These are made to suit the people and make life better for the particular community and this time need not to have anything with the shrine/alusi. These titles encourage brotherly relationship among the people. Other titles are "Ndi Ogbuefi" "The Cow Killer title" "Ndi

Ikenga" which means "The Ikenga title" "Okeofia""Ndi-Isiugo" "Ndi-Ezeugo""Ndi-Ezeani""Ndi-ozo Ezeani" etc.

Elders (titled elders)"Ichie"

Titled elders are only the eldest men, a man that is 50 years and above. In a family with three men (sons), it is the eldest of the three that will be selected to be a titled man 'ICHIE' it is only when a man qualifies the criteria for selection that he will be selected. Meek, C. (1937). "Law and Authority in a Nigerian Tribe" Pub. London

He must not be living irresponsible life; he must have conscience and must be healthy.

Elders (Titled Elders Cap/okpu)

The cap worn by the titled elders has a serious aim and objective which it stands for; they have a cap worn by the king's cabinet, others for the king, his advisers, etc.

Here, we want to discuss about the cap used to confer title in Igbo land. This cap reminds the bearer that he must live a responsible life, failure to do so will bring disaster upon his head. Nwosu, P. (2010), "The Age of Cultural Hybridization" A traditional bangle/aka is also given to a titled man, telling him that he must not collect bribe; the one worn on neck is to prevent him from living a promiscuous life, the one worn on the waist is to prevent him from living an irresponsible life, the staff he holds to, a symbol of authority. The walking stick symbol of power to rule. All the above instrument or materials are given to a titled man when he is taking an oath of allegiance in Igbo land and must have nothing to do with shrine/alxsi.

CORONATION OF A KING AND WHAT IT MEANS "Igwe"

As the Igbo's left the land of Israel, certain tradition which they are practicing today were learnt from them. The Israelites don't have a leader as president, this started when the people of Israel moaned and said to Samuel, "other countries have king but we don't have one". They pleaded with Samuel to give them a king. God became angry with the Israelites because he is the God of the Israelites. But God later gave them King Saul because of their wish for a king, we all saw in the Bible that this brought serious problem to the Israelites. After the Igbos came where they live today as Nigerians, some part of the Igbos institute king (Igwe), Obi etc. Aroh (2003) "However, there are some areas in Igbo land that had monarchical kingdoms, like Aguleri, Arochukwu, Nri, Onisha, Oguta and few others" but majority of the other Communities were usually governed and administered by a council of elders as it were in the land of the Israelites. Aroh E.C. (2003) stated that "the Igbos have no central government and administrative system prior to the coming of the Europeans" Although title holders were respected because of their accomplishments and capabilities, they were never revered as kings, but often performed special functions given to them by such assemblies. Law starts with the Umunna which is a male line of descent from a founding ancestor (who the line is sometimes named after) with groups of compounds containing closely related families headed by the eldest male member. The Umunna can be seen as the most important pillar of Igbo society.

Leadership is town by town, kindred by kindred kingdom by kingdom, despite all these; there are peace in the land until the people of Portuguese came in the 15th century and confer title to some people known as "warrant chief", and they were given gun to direct, guide and lead the Igbos. According to ATODO, and OBIORAH (2012)"Indirect rule was a complete failure in the East because of the absence of centralized system of administration and traditional institutions like the Emirs and the Obas in the other areas. Then Lugard and his administration created headache for themselves by appointing paramount chiefs". According to Okoli Donald Ofobuike and Eze Festus Emeka (2004) "In Northern and western parts of Nigeria, we had centralized political system and their existing political institutions were conducive for the operation of the Indirect Rule System. In the Eastern part of Nigeria, we did not have easily recognized ruler hence the British imposed 'Warrant Chiefs' on the people".

In the real culture of the Igbo, it is the responsibilities of the elder to lead, they have the final say in all matters.

ROLES OF A KING "IGWE" AND WHAT THIS TITLE STANDS FOR

The 'Igwe' is the head of all traditions; because of this, he must be familiar with all traditions of the Igbos, the boundary of the kingdom he is ruling, number of villages that make up his kingdom, number of kindred in his town or kingdom, the history of the land, the laws of the land, what and what are considered as taboo in the land. He must live in the kingdom where he rule, he must know the problem of his people, he must be able to speak their language, and must have a basic knowledge about administration. Some of the Igwes in Igbo land find it difficult to speak Igbo language, this is a big shame on the face of his people that, he conducts their meeting in English language; a king is not supposed to jump into any case and render judgment, it is the duty of the titled elders to judge any case.

The 'Igwe' means multitude/igwe mmadu. Democracy is the name. Because of this, the Igwe is not supposed to live a reckless life. A person expecting/hoping to be Igwe is to be patriotic, he must be God fearing, he must be ready to sacrifice his life for his people and must cherish the progress of his kingdom. Every town or kingdom should have rules and regulations guiding the igweship.

'Igwe' should not be a do or die affair, it is the highest form of cultural authority; this means that before any man becomes 'Igwe', he must have been a titled man. 'Igwe' must be someone accepted/selected by the people. He is not any type of person. Any person fighting over ruler ship of Igwe should not be given any chance to be Igwe in any part of Igbo land.

If the Igwe or rulers of the people does not know the right thing to do, there will be problem. The white men organized Nigeria in the year 1898; they were angry when Nnamdi Azikiwe and others ask them to go back to their country, that we want independent. Okoli D. Ofobuike and Eze F. Emeka (2004) The Aba women Riot 1929-1930 demanded that "all white men should go to their country so that the land in this area might remain as it was many years ago before the advent of the white man. Their annoyance with the Igbos because of what Azikiwe and others did was to give ammunition to the wrong people to become rulers of the Igbos. This was seen in 1914 when the Igbos, Hausas and Yorubas was amalgamated which was difficult because of difference in culture, religion and belief. According to Atodo P. A. and Obiorah C.C (2012) Sir Abubarkar Tafawa Balewa, stated in 1948, "Since 1914, the British government has been trying to make Nigeria into one country, but the Nigeria people themselves are historically different in their background, in their religious beliefs and customs and do not show in themselves any sign of willingness to unite". Even till date in Igbo land the Igweship is like ozu nwa onyeocha.

CHAPTER EIGHT
God is with the Igbos forever

Jesus Christ came into this world to spread the good news and to save mankind in the land of the Jews. In the world today, the majority of the Igbo people are Christians, although many also retain belief in their traditional religion. Over half of the Christians are Roman Catholic; the Igbos produces more men ordained as priests in the world today. British rule brought about changes in Igbo culture, such as the introduction of Warrant Chiefs as Eze where there were no such monarchies. Christian missionaries introduced aspects of European ideology into Igbo society and culture, sometimes shunning parts of the culture. Aspects of Igbo culture such as construction of houses, education and religion changed following colonialism. The tradition of building houses out of mud walls and thatched roofs ended as the people shifted to materials such as cement blocks for houses and zinc roofs. Roads for vehicles were built. Buildings such as hospitals and schools were erected in many parts of Igbo land. Along with these changes, electricity and running water were installed in the early 20th century. With electricity, new technology such as radios and televisions were adopted, and have become commonplace in most Igbo households. We could recall that Igbo people have produced bronzes from as early as the 9th century, some of which have been found at the town of Igboukwu, Anambra state. Pottery dated to around(2500) BCE showing similarities with later Igbo work was found at Nsukka, along with pottery and tools at nearby Ibagwa;

In July 6th, 1967, the Hausas threatened to wipe away the Igbo, but God was with the Igbos. The Hausas could not fulfill what they said even after 14th January 1970 and till today the Igbos are the pillars of our country Nigeria. All the effort of Obafemi Awolowo, Yakubu Gowon and the rest of them to disintegrate the Igbos as one were all in vain. They divided the eastern Nigeria into two- East-Central and South Central in May 27th, 1967. As stated by Atodoand Obiorah(2012) "The reasons for the creation of 12 states, according to Col. Gowon, were to remove fear of domination of any tribe by a larger one and ostensibly to crush the secessionist spirit of the Eastern Region from the Federation". Later the creation of Anambra and Imo state by Gen. Murtala Mohammed. The Capital at Calabar which was the first British colony (1842) was taking to Lagos in1963 and from Lagos to Abuja in December (12, 1991).

ELEMENTS OF DISINTEGRATION IN IGBO LAND

All the above points and the ones below are some of the things that lead to disintegration among the Igbos. See F.C. Okoli (2000) Later Igbo tribe was divided into five states and they includes Enugu, Anambra, Imo, Abia, Ebonyi, not talking of Ikwere Rivers, Igbo-Ekwurekwu Cross Rivers and Anioma Delta. This sharing of State brought division among the Igbos. That is why an Igbo will ask a fellow Igbo which State are you from? Is it Anambra or Enugu or Imo etc. The Ebonyi State will claim to be the head of the Igbo tribe and Abia will say I am the original.

It is selfishness that will make an Igbo to discriminate against a fellow Igbo simple because they are not from the same State. We beg all of us (Igbos) people of Israel living in the Eastern part of Nigeria let that spirit of hatred and division planted among us not deceive us, we are one despite our different states. Soon, we will have up to 30 states in Igbo land or more, do you know where you will belong then? So please if anything happens to any state in Igbo land, let all feel the pains and show concern. According to Editorial Board Bigard Theological Studies (2005) "Though the original contact of the Igbo with the white men and the events that followed have been said to lay the foundation of conflicts in Igbo society".

CHAPTER NINE
SECOND IN COMMAND (THE ELDEST TITLED MAN) (ONOWU)

The eldest titled man is known as the (Onowu), he is the second in command and high judge, because if the king is out of the town or country or dead after one year, it is the eldest man that will see that everything is put back in place both the organization for a new Igwe.

If a new 'Onowu' is selected, in the absent of the old one, the old Onowu becomes the (Ikenga)

Deputy To the King/Okpala, or Obi:

The deputy to the king in any kingdom is usually the head of the titled men, and the leader of Elders, he is not like other titled men, some called him Okpara, or Ononaobi, or Okpara he is the ofo bearer, He is God made. Aroh (2003) added that "Judicial administration in Igbo land starts from the family, Cases were brought to Okpala, he may decide to call in the Umuada or Umuokpo" He is also the head of coronation or title apart from the king. A deputy to the king must be familiar with, all the history of the town; he must be some one that commands a lot of respect in Igbo land. Odukwe, M. (1999). "The Okpala Institution in Onitsha". If the king is in doubt of any case or issue, it is the deputy that will clarify him.

CHAPTER TEN
The Meaning of "Umuada na Umuokpu"
What is "Ada" or "Umu Okpu"?

"Umuokpu or Umuada" means any woman born in Igbo land. I.e. 'daughter of the soil' They have a lot of respect and dignity in their place. Any full-fledged woman will always join this group 'Ada' to do their thing. If she did not do it in some towns, she must do it the day she will be going to her husband's house." Umuada" is a status. What it shows is that one is old and a mature woman. In the event of marriage of a girl it is this group that brings her out for the husband. In some towns if you don't satisfy them, they may not bring out the woman being married for the husband to take home. And nobody can stop them from doing this since they are very rooted in that land.

The Work of "Ada/Umu Okpu"

"Umuokpu" in Igbo land has a lot of powers. If a particular person's case becomes difficult, it is this group that will confront the person and even tell him/her what to do. If a man maltreats his wife or kills her, it is this group that will go and fight for the woman. At times men may overlook some humiliating or degrading behaviour against women. It is the "Umuada" that will challenge the situation and eventually become victorious. For example, in the year 1929,"umu Ada" staged a protest, the first of its kind in Africa at Aba popularly called Aba women riot. This was as a result of high-handed rule of the colonial government on the people and forcing us to pay tax that was considered to be beyond the income of the people. If on the other hand it is found that it is the woman that maltreats the husband that the man cannot fight for himself, it is this Umuada that will come and fight for the man.

Alualu
What is Alualu?
"Alualu" refers to women married from other places other than one's village or town; whereas the "Umuokpo" are those born in the town. The work of these women Alualu married from other places in a town is to see that peace reigns in the town. Some call them "Iyom"or inyom/nnwedi. If a woman is newly married; the first day she is married, this group will always receive her with songs and dances. This group is also referred to as "Nwunyedi". If a woman delivers a child, it is this group that will go to the hospital to escort her home with dances and songs joyfully. If a woman insults another woman, it is this group that will see to it that due punishment is given to the offender. "Alualu" help each other in different ways. They help in contributions/isusu, or to one who is bereaved, in cooking on any ceremony in which their member is carrying out, by fetching water, fetching firewood, washing clothes, clearing the bush, contributions, giving words of advice to their members for peace to reign in their families; praying together for their community to be good and helping out in various forms in any ceremony they are invited to help.

CHAPTER ELEVEN
Igbo Culture "Ejirimara Igbo"

After talking about **tradition**, which is the acts of a people over the years, it is time for us to talk about culture now. Culture of a people is about how people do their things. Things for which a particular people are known. It is very similar to custom. But custom precedes culture because it is those acts and practices over a period of time and handed over to younger generation that form the culture of a people. Igbo culture among others include language, the type of god we worship, our songs, dances, dressing, food and our burial pattern etc.

What Igbos Are supposed to Learn

Since we have known that Igbos are children of Israel, we have seen the good tradition of ours and also seen our lineage and from where we came and where we are going.

2. Where The Igbos are going

Our fore-fathers left the land of Israel because of the problems in Israel; it was worshiping of the idols and other sins that ignited the anger of God, then there was a war in the land of the Jews. We have explained these at the beginning of the book. It is disobedience to God that brought about all these problems. Read your Holy Bible and also buy the music "Igbo Amaka"2014, or Sampio music 2016 which was produced by Bijec music international, songs by Chief, Ben Ugochukwu Ikeokwu. Play this music and listen to them. One of it says: "Since we have realized ourselves, let us go back and face our God, let us know that all Igbos are one, let us know that we

are from the same father and mother"
Let us clear all traits of abomination and curses in the land we are occupying now. If we do this and call on God with one voice, I tell you, He will answer us.

What is clearing the Land?

When one commits an abomination, the abomination is cleared with some rituals and there is peace again in the land. Many Igbo people have committed a lot of abomination and topped it over and over again, yet still popped out their eyes like a rat that is flung to the ground looking for one to point accusing finger at.

Many Igbo people learnt to join cultic societies from other races that is from the west. They learnt worshipping idols from other tribes while they were travelling from Egypt. Igbos do not regard wasting of blood as anything because of what they learnt from other nations around. In our relationship with the whites, it is not only the Igbos that the west forced to speak English language, but today, other races have learnt that he who comes into the world, will go back to the place he came from. Again, he who is eating food is supposed to be watching his stomach. Moreso, when a hen Is gathering food, it should be looking sideways for possible danger. The other two races held firm to their languages and gods but the Igbos who are supposed to be wiser than the others are stupid; have made themselves naked and are walking about without any shame whatsoever. Not even some of the leaders of Igbos are not asking questions as to what to do so that Igbos will eventually reach home.

Clearing the ground is clearing those things that brought about God's curse so that they will be removed from where the Igbos is living today. Take a look at LEVITICUS 20;22- The Lord said, "Keep all my laws and commands, so that you will not be rejected by the land of Canaan, into which I am bringing you. Do not adopt the customs of the people who live there; I am driving out those pagans so that you can enter the land. They have disgusted me with all their evil practices". Some Igbos think that since they are educated, that they know everything. There are the people who also mislead many Igbos today by telling the youths (men) to spare the shrines as they (the shrines) are going to be a source of their knowledge in future. You can see that today the youths i.e. our boys and girls have started clearing all the shrines in the land thinking erroneously that this is a way of salvation. God will ask the Igbo leaders questions about these souls that are being lost, because they are not doing what they are supposed to do like clearing the land. God does not accept nine and half but the whole ten to show the other nations why He is the God of Israel and that of Igbo land.

What Will the Igbos Do?

All the towns in Igbo land should take this seriously. They ought to convene a meeting, either during New Yam festival or during Christmas or Easter periods. If the Igbo race do their part which is clearing and ridding the Igbo land of all the shrines scattered everywhere, that of secret cult is personal war since it is not written on anyone's face i.e., it cannot be seen with the eyes. If the Igbos do this and call on God with one voice, God will know how to deal with the ones we cannot see.

The Mystery

God cannot do for a man what that man can do for himself. What God will do for a man are those ones he couldn't do for himself. This should be done by the people at a time but whereby it becomes difficult, you can start doing this on individual basis, from there to the family and to the town. This will be appreciated by God.

Those who Scatter Igbos and the Enemies of the Igbos

These people are increasing in Igbo land and this has resulted in the inability of the Igbos to love themselves. Read genesis 6:4, you will see the fallen angels that took flesh, married, begot children just for the purpose of scattering the world. Do you know them or who they are today. Look very well to know how many they are. They can come to be your brothers, sisters or your friends. They can wear the look of leaders both in the church, in your town, state or country but how you will know them is the type of fruit they bear.

How They are Known

They will tell you that committing evil is nothing or that there is nothing like sin. They will also tell you that whoever is protected by God should also protect himself with this or that which implies that man should not leave himself empty handed. They will also tell you that God's law is not all that is important, that poverty is a curse, that God did not create men to suffer, that Idol worship or occult membership is good that there is nothing bad in it, that it is God that created all these adding that it is a way to progress. If you don't know them before, know that what they are concerned with is just things of this world and what is in the world alone. Heaven and God's laws are not important to them at all. They will mislead you or do you what will make you offend God if you do not hold yourself together.

Religious Practice

The God the Igbos worship in the land of Israel is only one God. Later devil and it's workers, those spirit that came into the world took the form of human beings and taught human beings how to disobey God, by worshiping them more than God. Let me ask a question? Assuming you gave birth to a child, brought him up, pay his school fees, and all the suffering involved in training the child and the child grows up and becomes a lawyer, or doctor and after training him and he grows up and starts seeing you as an old man that is of no use, he will take all the wealth you suffered to build up in your youth and dash them out to your enemy. How will you feel? Some people said that worshiping idols is the same with worshiping God, that there is only one God. And there are other ways you can look for God like: moon, sun, water, stream, earth, stone, hills and valley, animals and human beings, gold, short wears, idols, man-made gods. Editorial Board Bigard Theological Studies (2005) some use churches like false prophets thinking they are worshiping the true God but they are simply servants to the devil. They will be deceiving people that they worship the true God.

Good Ways of Worship God

In the year 01/01/AD God sent His only begotten son to come to this world and teach the people life in the world and the best way to worship God. The name of the son of God is Jesus Christ. It is not the way you think that is the best, but it is that way that our Lord Jesus Christ teaches that we who live in this world are to worship him. We are remembering the birth of our Lord Jesus Christ up to 2016AD that we are in today. All creatures waited for his coming, When he was born, they started counting one, two, three and four until today that is 2016 the year of Christ. Before he came, what the world was writing was BC which means Before Christ. After he had come, the world started writing AD (Anno Domino), which means 'in the year of the Lord'. So if you want to worship God it is no longer how you think or how those that have not understood think, but how the Lord wants. Before He ascended to heaven he sent 12 of his disciples and made Simon Peter the head. Believe this and have life.

This is the true religion the Igbos should accept, which is the culture and tradition of the Igbos. Whoever strays from this way of life is lost.

CHAPTER TWELVE

Singing

Singing is a profoundly human action. It expresses not merely our emotions, but the attitude of our whole human personality. The act of producing musical sounds with the voice, and augments regular speech by the use of sustained tonality, rhythm, and a variety of vocal techniques. A person who sings is called a singer or vocalist. Singers perform music (arias, recitatives, songs, etc.) that can be sung with or without accompaniment by musical instrument. Singing is often done in an ensemble of musicians, such as a choir of singers or a band of instrumentalists. Singing can be formal or informal, arranged or improvised.

The Igbos use song to praise God and their fellow human being. Harry Belafonte(1954).They use song to show happiness. Whenever the Igbos are celebrating, they sing song even when they are welcoming visitors, or to praise a great person or to praise someone or to beg someone or to express the happiness of a group of people or village. Large, John W (February–March 1972).There are songs that express happiness. There are songs for worship; there are songs for judging people that is (criticism). There are songs for the marine spirit, for witchcraft. We must know which type of song and for which people and purpose before we join in such song.

Benefits from Singing Songs

Singing helps to awaken a depressed heart and gives healing. Singing song for God is called praises. Lucero, Jorge C. (1995. God likes it so much if you use a clean and righteous heart in singing it. The Igbos will say that it is sweeter than white yam. What God eat is only praises.

Phyllis Fulford; Michael Miller (2003).Praising his name because he is greater than all is all that is important.. When you are doing this without sitting on anybody position or head, not carrying anger for anybody, this will make God to be happy. It will make God to forgive and bless you and other people. Whoever that sing praises to God always have favour from God. The type of song you play or sing always show the type of person you are. There are people that sing but they are having pain in their heart. Some people are singing what they call song but there is pain in their heart, like bitter leaf and painful like pepper. Levitin, Daniel J. (2006).This kind of music is not gainful in the presence of God. Singing good song brings favour to the person singing it and happiness. McKinney, James C (1994).It also gives the person or those singing it the salvation and joy in the heart. This is how praises also gives salvation to the person singing it, happiness, holiness, protection, deliverance, repentance and upliftment. Through this you will be able to pursue devil and his workers.

After singing, you can start praising the person with names and when you praise person in the congregation of people the person may start doing what he did not want to do before. At the same time, after singing, and praising God. This will make Him to come down and do a lot of miracles in our lives.

Dancing

Dancing is one of the tradition of the Igbos. When a traditional ceremony is being done in Igbo land, we have dances of different types. Some musicians will come like "Egwu ekpiri", Egwu ogba Igbadara, Egwu Umuokpu, Egwu umuokorobia, Egwu Umuagboohobia, Egwu umuagbara, Egwu echichi, Egwu umuaka, we have some music like Egwu Ogbanje, Egwu owummiri, Egwu ogbanajirija, Egwu ndi amusu, egwu ndi ogba na nkpuru, egwu mmanwu, Egwu omenikoro, Egwu uraga, Egwu mgbadike, Egwu ichoku, Egwu jamba, Egwu Oganigwe, Egwu enyiaga na mkpa, Egwu Odanahaonu, Egwu kwari kwata, Egwu ijere, Egwu ngala. Egwu onwu, Egwu ihunanya, Egwu-ufie, Egwu Abia etc.

Any dance has reasons for their different kinds. Nathalie Comte. "Europe, 1450 to (1789) there are dances that are used to praise God, Satan, distraction, heart break and love. Some music are used in remembering what happened in the past like "Egwu agha, Egwu onuma. Sondra Horton Fraleigh (1987).Whenever they are singing and dancing music they are shown through the way the music is played and things used in playing it, and the place it is being played. Bad music don't give God glory; for this reason, it is not all music that we should watch or join those dancing it. Like the Igbos normally say "Asi Dike yaagbana abia, O kaba ndi ogburu". Ames, David. Ethnomusicology. A Comparative Examination". Vol. 17, No. 2. (May, 1973), pp. 250-278. The birds of a feather flock together. The way you do things is how the people see you.

Igbo and their mode of Dressing

As we explained at the beginning of this book, that the Igbo's look smart and good. It is true that before we become developed today, the Igbo's were wearing kalico clothes because there were no clothes. It looked like the Igbos were naked men; they wore and tied wrapper around their waist to cover their nakedness. Some wore animal skin or leaves gotten from plant that they used. Women wore things called jude, peteri etc. The church and the white people brought development, they brought clothes to us too. We are supposed to be wearing decent clothes that make us look decent. In addition, our first parents Adam and Eve started wearing cloth to cover their shame. They heard the voice of God, they hid because they were naked. God now helped them by sewing cloth for them to cover their nakedness. GENESIS 3.21 .So this is showing that it is to cover our nakedness that we wear cloth, not to show nakedness.

Types of clothes that the Igbos supposed to wear

Because the Igbos don't know themselves again, even where they come from and where they are going, They are practicing other people's culture and tradition, that is the type of cloth they wear and wear more than the people they imitate. Deuteronomy 21;5- "Women are not to wear men's clothing, and men are not to wear women's clothing; the LORD your God hates people who do such things". It is true that it is not all the Igbos that do this abomination. What are their parents doing when their wards are wearing those cloths? Where are they? Are these people not from the village of Igbo land? What are the village rulers doing when they hear of this kind of situation. People like the Chiefs, the crown people, Umuada/Umuokpu, the P.Gs, the Igwes, Igbo Governors, the wives of the governors. Priests and church leaders what are you doing? "My child is greater than me is falsehood and cunning which amounts to self-deceit. We know that the mad person is not ashamed of himself. It is his brother or sister that the shame go to.

The reason why we wear cloth is to cover our nakedness but those people from the fallen spirits like showing their nakedness. This shows that those whom these spirits gave birth to are more than those that human beings gave birth to. All these are not supposed to surprise you because end time is approaching. As we explained at the beginning of this book. That the spirit came and took flesh dwelt among us; they gave birth to their children in the world, and their intention is to gain souls for their father who is the devil. There is a serious demarcation between those given birth to by these spirits and those given birth to by human beings. For example those who are real human beings, when they are up to eight years are always ashamed when they are naked and would not allow anybody to see their nakedness especially, outsiders. This shows that they are from good lineage. Good lineage/stock do not allow the cloth they are wearing inside to be shown outside. The clothes they wear cover their body very well and give them space like a child of God created in his own image. That is what it means for you to know the child of who you are and where you come from.

The Types of food that the Igbos Eat

52.   Igbos have many food that they eat which is gotten from God. They have different types of food like: yam, tapioca or African salad, cocoyam, breadfruit, meat, fish, vegetables, plantain, banana etc. Basden, G. T.(2013).
Among the Ibos of Nigeria: 1912. Routledge. p. 45.
These varieties of food are found in the place where we are born and serve as the best food to us. Eating other people's food too much is not good. So for this reasons, eating food that is in your locality is good for your body, for long life and prosperity, and help you live as long as God wants you to live.

Why the Igbos don't eat all animals

Many towns in Igbo land don't eat some animals in Igbo land like rabbit, some fishes, sheep, monkey, python, some snake, snail, tortoise, cocoyam etc. Some towns avoid some of these animals because they are sacred. One strange thing about the killing of any of these animals is that the defaulter will be forced to perform funeral rites in respect of the animal killed or face death sentence. If a man go outside his chamber, he will call a priest that will hold land for him until he comes back. Levi C. N. and kem Fab-Ukozor (2003): 150. Any animal they use to do the ritual/charms for that man is for the protection and will not be eaten by him. Anyahuru, Israel; Ohiaraumunna, Tom (2009).The high priest will tell him not to eat that animal again including his generation to come.

If there is war, or that the village want to prepare themselves for such war, any animal used for such rituals will not be eaten by them again for that generation. Some are animals used in the foundation of shrines or villages this is showing that they and that spirit are in covenant all through their life.

This results in going to the church and worshipping idols in our society today some who have a lot of problems today are as a result of those animals that their fore-fathers gave to the spirits in covenant, which this generation abandoned and say that they are going to church. Uzor Peter C. (2004).You will ask in the church if you have rejected devil and its work? You say yes, while you have not rejected it. Why because you accept Satan through accepting the covenant that your forefathers had with Satan and his agents. By accepting not to be eating all these meat used in that covenant between their gods and their land. God is a jealous God. He requires all from us.

What Obtains In our Land (Odinala)

The Igbos have a lot that came with our lands or our inheritance. So many people misunderstand what is called inheritance/odinala and the explanation of it. That is what we obtain where God created us, to help the people living along that side to live long life. It is how their land behaves and produces, not shrine/alusi. Morton, W. R. G. (1956)."God, man and the land in a Northern Ibo village-group" There are some land which produce food more than fruit, there are land which produces breadfruit but palm tree cannot grow there, there are lands that grow cassava; there are lands for food, sandy, humus soil, clay soil, there are land where we cultivate fruit, there are land that do well in cocoyam but yam don't grow there. There are lands that don't grow anything at all etc. Land content is what is in the land; it is how the land behave that is "ODINALA". Odinala is natural, not shrine/alusi. Also as we said in the beginning, some lands are very hot that anybody who lives there always experience sudden death and problem until they park out from there. Uzukwu, Elochukwu Eugene (2012).There are other lands like holy land, desert, 'ozara' land that grow trees used in building houses, or plant used in producing drugs in different types. There are white sand land, stone land etc. There are lands where people who live there are always big, there are lands where people who live there are always dwarf, there are land where people who live there "na ada ibi", have swollen genitals, there are some lands where people who live there are always tall or fat, there are strong land that people who live there are always strong etc.

What causes all this is that God created each land differently. It is those that live in the land that destroy the land and it will becomes a disturbance to them if you take another person's land by force or cunningly. It will cause the land to be angry. Spilling of blood, doing abominable thing, against the land will be a curse on those people or the person that did it, until it kills them all. That is why we hear that one behaves like one being pursued by the land "onye ana na-akpa". The land will continue to pursue them until they all die. You cannot do this one by power. Olupona, Jacob K.; Nyang, Sulayman S.; Kalu, Ogbu U. (1993).The answer is that anybody or group of people that committed a taboo, will confess it and the abomination shall be expiated so that the land will be cool again.

In the land of the Jews, there is a place that anybody that commits abomination will be crucified, when they thought that Jesus Christ committed abomination, by saying that he and the God the father are one and the same. To add salt to injury, he added that he will give them his body to eat and his blood to drink. They agreed to crucify him on the cross as a person who has committed abomination. They have a bush for that in the land of the Jews - a place where that person will stay until they clear his abomination. In the land of the Jews there are lands where those that are sick stay, you will leave where other people are and go to that land and stay. Our forefathers came with that tradition to our land today where they lived in different parts of Nigeria. They call it evil forest, ajo-ohia, agu-nwijam, agu-njo.

What Obtains In a Family (OdinaObi/Odunobu)

What obtains in a particular compound or in a generation. Akaegbu, John Ofoegbu(1991).This is why Igbo people normally ask a lot of questions before they do anything. Such things like choosing a priest, the king, town's representative, marriage, Ozo-title-taking, Ichies, king's representative/Onowu etc. This has two faces:

The Good Side

If a man lived a good life in this world and later died, it is possible that he did not enjoy all his suffering when he was alive "Ekelechi" or "Akara aka" i.e. one's luck is the thing that determines how each compound is going to be. Ilogu, Edmund(1974). It may be that when blessings will start coming, it will be in the hands of his children or children's children in another generation. That is why any child in that family whenever he touches anything in that house it will be a blessing, if he goes out with other children to fetch fire wood, his own will be more, if they go to hunt for pears, snail, oil bean, yam, palm kernel, he will do it better than others and it will surprise other children. It may even be that other children are taller and advanced in age than Ugoo. When Ugoo and other children have gone to fetch something, others may not see it but Ugoo will see it because God has decided to bless his generation in the particular family. Ejizu, Christopher I. (1986).When this happens, others will ask him, why is it that you see more than us, we all passed here we did not see anything and now that you pass you saw it.

Sometime when they go out for hunting, it will be Ugochukwu that will see and kill all the animals they will hunt for, even though he is not the eldest of all. If he comes into the school he will be special because he is intelligent, sometimes he makes too much noise but he is always the best. He always takes first, second or third position. If he finishes his education or starts learning hand work, it will be like there is another thing following him. Where he is selling with his fellow children, it will be like there is another thing following him, some will start asking him if he is using any charm or where did he get it, if he is a civil servant all you will be hearing is promotion, even if they deceived him and he goes for the ritual, he/she will still progress. Even if he did not do any ritual, he will still progress. This is because his blessing is from the compound/OdinaObi. The power of the compound is not only about money, it can be in form of prophecy. Onunwa, Udobata R. (2010)He may be given a power of work or protection that no spirit or human being can do anything to him. He may be prayerful or not prayerful but whatever he says must happen. He may be given knowledge, intelligence, decision-making, leadership, healing or thinking out what others cannot think of etc. This kind of person should know that this entire gift is not for him alone, that he is supposed to use it and help others no matter what the world will say.

Bad Side

On the other side if any man lived bad life and later died, at times the misfortune start when the man is still alive. The coming generation will start suffering for what he did. Sufferings like backwardness, bareness, inability to sell and make money, constant trouble, lack of promotion, sudden death, early death, bad luck etc. people like this may be taken to a herbalist, secret society, or mushroom churches for something to start going well with him, but all is in vain, This means that the curse is in that generation as a result of what his mother and father or forefather had done/odinobu. Some will say that they are under curse or charm/'Agwu'. Isichei, Elizabeth Allo (1977). They will now look for the destruction of what was done but all will be vain. This is just what they will do to console somebody who did not have hope again.

What are we going to do In This situation? /odinobu or odinaobi

The only thing we can do in this situation is for you to start living a good life. Since it is a curse to sin or to do bad thing or to commit abomination. Sin of one's father or forefather is the cause of all these problems, so they supposed to start living a good life. Ogbaa, Kalu (1995). So that the person's children and his next generation will not see what they are seeing. Anything that you know that is sinful don't do it, follow the good road, keep your heart clean like the heart of a child of God. The person should believe in Jesus Christ. Through one's struggle, prayers and fasting. God may change your position.

CHAPTER THIRTEEN
What Is A Curse?

A curse is what destroys a generation of people in a compound or a family. This is as a result of what is where they are not supposed to be or things gotten from annoying God.

Things that are where they are not supposed to be

One who gives out a girl with pregnancy in marriage secretly. This pregnant girl becomes a curse to those that have married her.

He or those who took a child whose mother they did not pay the price for or marry officially either by theft, by cunning or secretly so that the child becomes theirs. The child is a curse to them.

The land, town, wherever or the compound where there is a shrine/idol. This is a curse to these places mentioned.

Different forms of curses

Whatever is stolen and where it is kept. Others are money gotten from prostitution or sexual relationship, stolen money, obtaining by tricks or 419, blood money, money from kidnapping. He or She who has this money and whatever he does with it. He who sacrifices to idol or wherever those things used in the sacrifices are kept.

He who steals the money used in offering to God. The money is also a curse. He who forcefully takes something that belongs to another person because he is in a higher position, or stronger than the person. He who makes love to a child 'ikwa ikwo' or sleeps with an animal 'Igba inyo' a man sleeping with a fellow man and woman doing the same 'Ikwa Inyo' These are everlasting curses.

Things gotten from provoking God

Things gotten from provoking God have explained itself but now let us give a little more explanation.

A person who establishes a church by himself, self-acclaimed prophet, healing, evil money and wealth, etc. all these are curses forever, and whatever thing these money is used for. All the people that visit a false prophet, or accept his/her prayer, his medicine or believe in his vision or prophecy, whether you know or you don't know the person or the people. These are curses but the person that did not know, his spiritual disconnection from the entanglement is easier.

The money given for the spilling of blood, the phone use in doing that, computer, gun, knife, motor, and all the money use in kidnapping etc. They are all everlasting curses.

Question: Can somebody curse?

Answer: Yes, somebody can curse as a result of pains and heartbreak. But it is not advisable because at times, it backfires.

Question: If somebody curses another person, is it God or Satan that will go for the fight?

Answer: We know that the devil does not hear 'save' but 'kill' but God has the final judgment.

Question: Is it all the curses that somebody places on fellow human beings that happen?

Answer: No. This is because human beings do not know everything. For example, a person may think that something is like this but it is the other way eventually. In such a case, if we place a curse on a person, like that, it brings blessings to that person and brings destruction to the person that cursed him because it is God that has the last word.

Question: Are human beings supposed to go for vengeance?

Answer: Human beings are not supposed to go for vengeance. No human being is supposed to go for revenge because God says that we should leave vengeance for him.

Question: Why are human beings not supposed to go for revenge despite all the ugly things we see today?

Answer: Human beings are not supposed to go for vengeance because it is only to God that anybody whose heart has been broken should cry to because He is the only one that knows the best way and the right time to pay for whatever one has committed.

Question: Some people say that since the work of the devil and his agents is to kill and destroy, is it better to run to Satan and His agents who kills faster?

Answer: It is not better to run to Satan who kills faster, instead of going to God who takes time because of His mercy? No, running to Satan to kill people fast shows that you are evil yourself, no matter what that person has done to you, how big it is, forgetting that you, yourself is a sinner too, and that some conditions may be to try your faith. Let

God be the judge in this case.

What is outcast? Or 'OSU'

i. Outcast is somebody who ran to or embraced the shrine for protection because of fear, mal-treatment or protection from people stronger than him.

ii. They are the people or the person that have been bought and given to a shrine/alusi.

iii. Child of the shrine/Nwa-Alusi or the daughter of the shrine. i.e. he or she is owned by the shrine whether himself or herself or people dedicated him/her to the shrine or idol. Most of this people that are being called outcast/Osu today, don't know when this happened but they are called the generation of outcast today. Outcast is one of the traditions of the Igbo that is not even supposed to be talked about today. Like the killing of the twins have stopped today, together with anybody or any child that grows the upper teeth first, or anybody whose stomach swells, in the same way the issue of Osu caste system is supposed to have died. No town in Igbo land is supposed to talk about it again. All Igbo sons and daughters are children of God, outcast for God, Jewish people, children of Israel, those chosen by God all over the world to be his own in a special way. Hence, all Igbo sons and daughters are God's outcast. Anybody that calls a child of God, a child of the shrine/alusi has committed the greatest abomination.

Taking an Oath

Question: What type of oath can one take as a result of high level of allegations and wickedness in the world today?

Answer: If condition becomes too hard that there is

nothing to do again, you will approach any priest for them to direct you as the holy spirit wants.

Question: In case I did not accept what he explained due to the wickedness against me or my family or my town?

Answer: The last but not the least is taking an oath with the bible before God administered by the Priest, who will wear a red vestment to show that something is going to happen.

Question: Is it only a Priest that conducts this oath?

Answer: Yes, because this the way they handle it in the whole Igbo land in the earliest times, even from the land of Israel.

Question: Some say that bible does not kill somebody, that it is written by the foreigners and it is also an ordinary book?

Answer: This is not true but due to very poor understanding or due to their low mentality. Bible is the only book on earth today containing only the wisdom of God. It is the book written by God himself through an ordinary human being, but everything written in it are full of life and power, that means it kills and also has killed many people. Saying that bible does not kill is like saying that God is not powerful; saying this is provoking God. Remember that everything you use in taking an oath can kill because God is in everything He created. Seeking for help elsewhere is attracting curse and destruction to yourself.

REINCARNATION

Question: Can a Person Reincarnate?

Some Igbos have traditionally believed in reincarnation, ilo-uwa. Ogbuene, Chigekwu G. (1999)People are believed to reincarnate into families that they were part of while alive. Uzor Peter C. (2004).Rucker Walter C. (2006)

Answer: They believe this because of what they see and what they hear; it did not start today, because when Jesus was on earth, some Jewish people came to him and asked him about reincarnation. He answered them plainly that one cannot reincarnate.

Question: But why do people talk about reincarnation?

Answer: It is because they don't believe that Jesus Christ is the son of God and He is God himself. If somebody believes that Jesus is God and he was created by God himself and the whole world was also created by God, then how can we and God who create us be in contention over who created the other. What led some people to have this kind of belief is the work of devil and evil things in the world today.

Work of Devil

We explained before that some evil spirit took flesh and gave birth to people in this world and are still increasing in numbers as real human beings are procreating and increasing. GENESIS 6,1 to 5.Because so many people don't know something like this, it is like a surprise to them that a new child can talk and say that he reincarnated or an adult at the point of his death saying that he will reincarnate in his next world

Answer to this is that some who are looking for the fruit of the womb will go to any length to have a child. Some can sacrifice to the water, bush, grave etc. When these occur, it is a great chance for devil and their kingdom to come as a child or baby in the woman's womb so that the woman will have a baby. If we continue to write on this, it will be endless. It is due to lack of patience and disbelief in the word of God that give the devil and his agents the opportunity to lead people astray.

Can a Dead Person Come Out Again?

Answer: A dead person has no power of his own except that God gave him chance to send important message, because of some important issues or the love one has for a fellow human being like husband, wife, children and friend etc. A dead person has few days to deliver these important messages like 'I am going', 'Be in peace', 'tell somebody this', 'this is how this thing is' After those few days, the dead person has no power again to deliver messages. Ebelebe, Charles A.(2009).The living ones can intercede for him in prayers. If God Almighty decides He can still give chance for the person to go and deliver message in the world again.

What about those that Died Who Still Come out to destroy Things?

Anybody that died and comes out to destroy things are those that are not good people. They are the evil that are like human beings that gave their life to the devil when they were alive, all their efforts are bad things, but they have a short time on earth.

CHAPTER 14
What is Ofo

Ofo is described as a staff of authority; an insignia of office. This staff represents power. It is the dignity of the people or town. This short stick is from a plant called ofo that grows in the bush from which this symbolic stick is gotten. Before it becomes a staff of authority or power. It is given certain pronouncements and rituals. According to Mbaebie Joyce (2009) "Their sacred staff of office, called the OFO, symbolized the authority of the ancestors and was venerated as the embodiment of the supernatural world and all the spirits of the ancestors" It is a decision of somebody, kindred, village or town accord in the piece of wood respect and dignity which applies also to wherever it is kept. Ofo must not be made of the ofo tree but whatever the people choose to serve as ofo to them. Ofo is kept at the "Obu/Obi" which is a special house within the compound. It can be kept in this 'obu' in the palace of the king or at the 'obu' of the eldest in the compound or village. They gather there from time to time to meet and discuss. Not everybody is permitted to touch it. According to Levi Chinaka N. and Nkem Fab-Ukozo (2003) Nevertheless, ofo plays the same role wherever they exist. It is a highly sacred instrument of worship in which case, one who is not pure in the traditional sense cannot tamper with it. Not all the time that they bring it out. And women don't touch it. Only when things are challenging like in times of war, taking an oath, in time of peace and in time of a blessing etc. Emeka (1998)

How to Produce Staff of Authority (Ofo)

An upright man cuts ofo stick and prays over it. This prayer signifies uprightness and holiness of life.

This man will always avoid evil things. When things are challenging, he brings out the staff and declares to God that he has his truth in the staff, that earth should bear him witness. Cole, Herbert M. (1982)He says that he does not do any evil and does not go against anyone. Emeka (1998) submits that: "the symbol of the collective values and the collective spirit of a kinship or family group ofo invariably domiciles in the house of the eldest male (Di-okpala) who uses it to pray, to bless or to curse in the name of the family group". Then he will touch the staff on the ground, if there is any spirit or anybody holding his position or share working against him they will start having problems because God hears the prayer of a righteous man. Uzukwu, Elochukwu Eugene (2012).But if somebody like this does not fulfill the promise of righteousness, once he touches the staff on the land and making those declarations, he will experience more hardship than before and this can even lead to death.

If the righteous man dies, his children will keep this staff of their father or father's father and respect it and keep the laws of cleanliness and holiness. Whenever things are challenging, when he strike the staff on the ground, the same thing that happened during their father or their father's father will still happen.

Giving Somebody a Staff of Authority (OFO)

Giving someone a staff of authority means that he should not commit any evil thing because he has been given power to do great things. Oriji, John. "Sacred Authority in Igbo Society". Page 115

If such a person has been doing evil things before in his

life, after praying for him and giving him any symbolic object like ofo stick, staff, cap, hand fan, bangle, and cloths etc. all these things given to him will not work anything for him. Isichei, Elizabeth Allo (1977).Anything giving to him stands for the staff of that village, family, their Local Government that gave the staff. Ilogu, Edmund (1974)But once he starts living a good life after giving him the staff, the staff will work for him. Sometimes there is no symbolic object given to him, but if only it is prayer that is said for him it represents the staff effectively.

How to establish a shrine

Like we explained how shrine started on earth, this time we are to explain what the Igbo's called Shrine/alusi or how they establish it. **Alusi**, also known as **Arusi** or **Arushi**, are minor deities that are worshiped and served in Igbo mythology. There are lists of many different Alusi and each has its own purpose. When there is no longer need for the deity it is discarded.

In the olden days, due to so many years the Igbo have stayed which made them not to know the rightful way to serve God and in addition, due to their stubbornness to God which make them to leave the land of Israel, they started establishing and worshipping different gods with different names as other nations. The gods are so many which we are going to give you on DVD soon. One or few persons can establish a shrine/alusi. They would have in mind that the shrine will protect them, and where they live and also lead them successfully to wars, curing their sicknesses and also helping them to have bountiful farm work etc.

When any town or village calls a native doctor to come and

establish a shrine for them, that native doctor will tell them what they are to bring for the work.

In establishing this shrine, some use human beings for the sacrifice, while others may use cow, sheep, goat, snake, dog, monkey, etc. Gugler, Josef; Flanagan, William G. (1978). Anything that is used by the native doctor for the Alusi/shrine to be alive and effective must not be eaten by the man and their children forever. And such action will render the shrine ineffective. All these are specific manipulations designed by the devil to deceive even the so-called advanced mystics.

Most times, the whole town will be worshipping the shrine. Basden, G.T. (2013). "Among the Ibos of Nigeria". After some time, some villages or clans or families seek to go and establish their own. Those who have built their own houses or those who are running away from their town. They will carry less shrines and go to where they will settle down and live. This is why some shrines are bearing the same name today.

Some towns when they see and feel that a particular shrine in another town is powerful, they will go and take the shrine of that town to worship. Aguwa, Jude C.U. (1995). Because of this, at times, some will kill the medicine man that has come to do the medicine for them as that he will not do the same medicine to another people.

It is the village that owns the shrine that will decide where they will keep the shrine, the person that will be feeding the shrine 'Chief priest' and the day of worship, those that will fight for the shrine and also where the head will be placed etc. Opata, Damian Ugwutikiri (2009). the native doctor will tell them when to be sacrificing for the shrine otherwise it becomes ineffective. Williams, Ian (2005).Any animals used in establishing the shrine, whoever kills it will give it full human burial, otherwise that can destroy the medicine, "**ALUSI OGWU AGWORORO GI**".

There is a reason for establishing any shrine; some are for wars, security, taking an oath, killing somebody and also for wealth and farming etc.

What power is in the shrine?

As the creator of heaven and earth (God) explains, anybody that worships the alusi/shrine is like alusi/shrine he worships. He also explains that there is no power in the shrine. Ilogu, Edmund (1974). "Christianity and Ibo Culture". Brill Archive. pp. 23–24.Alusi is energized with the power of the fallen spirits.

A book we wrote called **"Power that leads"** there you will see where the different types of powers came from. There you will see what is casting medicine to somebody, power of time, power in the air, water, land, bush, tree, and human beings etc.

How Igbo prays in the Olden Days

Any Igbo man that wakes up in the morning, he washes his hands with water, his face, if he has altar he will go there to say his prayers. Some people plant "Ogbu tree" and call it "Ogbu Chi" which means the Ogbu tree that represents god. Chi - a sub-deity functioning as a personal, spiritual guide. Other places, other trees are planted and called "ndi Ichie" meaning, the ancestors etc. In front of that god, the staff (ofo) is placed, the traditional chalk is applied to it, bring out kola. Basden, G. S. (1966). "Among the Ibos of

Nigeria, 1912. Psychology Press: p. 109. The Chalk is used to make four strokes on the ground signifying four market days in Igbo land that represent one week. If the person is titled, he will strike the clay chalk as many times as he wants, that is based on the number of titles he has, before he throws the chalk to his god and applies some to his eyes for seeing and rubs on his face and legs etc. After all that, he picks up the kola and clears his throat and says that the day has broken. The first direction of his right hand and eye is in the cloud of heaven because Igbo believes that God lives in heaven. He might praise God with any name of his choice. Many Igbo dialects refer to God by names such as "Chukwu", "Chiokike", "Chineke" or "Obasi" before he starts calling those shrines he believes in and other ancestors and his forefathers that have already died because Igbo's believe that human being don't die but transits.

After calling the whole gods, he confesses his sins. After that, he lists those things that are important to him etc. after that, he breaks the kola; with his finger nails, removes the heart of the kola and throw it at the altar where he prayed. This means that those spirits he serves will eats part of the kola while he eats the other parts of it.

How some Igbos value alligator pepper

Alligator pepper is what some Igbos believe they can use for cleansing for somebody who has defiled himself. He will take the seed about three or more, parts them on his body and throws away. Then takes the one he will eat. He believes that with this purification exercise, that he is pure from sin after defiling himself before or from the defiling of another person.

What is an oath tree
What is oath neutralizing tree (Osisi Ndaru Iyi)

An oath tree is what they use in taking a false oath, because they know that the shrine/alusi has limited powers. This means that if a bad person goes to take an oath, he will look for a good oath-neutralizer against that shrine he wants to take oath of or go secretly to bribe those priests in charge of the shrine. But heaven and earth are bigger than all these things. There are many other trees that have powers like; anunuebe, inyime, oturu etc.

Chapter 15
WHEN ONE IS UNDER THE INFLUENCE OF A SPIRIT (AGWU)

This means when one is not able to locate his destiny. This at times leads to aimlessness. Sometimes this is the work of evil spirit. Whatever he lays his hands on will be scattered. He cannot indulge in any meaningful hand work or trade. What they normally do for such a person is to establish an 'agwu' altar or shrine of his own. Eboh, Simeon Onyewueke (2004).The medicine man who will do this will teach the person what and what to provide which may not take reasonable amount of money.

After all this, the native doctor will call on some shrines and invoke different types of spirit to come and stand at the place of the altar of sacrifice. In other words, this is a process of projecting a certain demon to a person, who may be quickened to manifest in action later. After all these he will plant a tree called 'ogirishi' or he will put native pot or plantain in other to appease those wicked spirits disturbing and scattering the person's things, but the truth is that it does not solve the problem because your enemy who hates you, will not do any good thing for you. Spinage, Clive (2012).Again one who is in bondage, cannot lose another person in bondage too. There is no good thing he can do for you. Answer to the person possessed by this spirit is for children of God to rescue him from the hand of the evil ones and his enemy through prayers of deliverance then they help him to locate his destiny. The spirit of 'agwu' most often possess men. There are however few cases of women being possessed.

WHAT DOES QUEEN MEAN/EZE NWANYI

Whenever a lady or a girl is in the form of a possessed human being, they call such person names like this: woman, a re-incarnated person, a soothsayer, one from the water, from the air, ogbanje etc. wicked jezebel, whatever she lay her hands on does not work, she will be going around with men, even if she gets married; she will not be in her husband's house; she will not value her children if she has some, she will be going like a rejected person. In a bid to help her, her people might take her to the people who do rituals to the water, native doctor that work for her, or to fake prophets.

These people will eventually lead such a person to different demonic altars for solution. This will also result in working for the spirit or demon. But all these are no solutions. The solution to the person in such condition is to take her to the true people of God to pray for her and deliver her before she will look for her destiny/akara aka.

What we should know

We should know that God does not give anybody a gift to worship the devil and those that work for the Devil. Nor does he give anybody the gift to worship devil and alusi/shrine since he said that anybody that worship devil will go to hell fire. He is a jealous God that does not want his creatures to give his glory to another created being other than Himself. There is nothing like I have a call to serve alusi, or being possessed by the spirit of agwu as one's destiny, re-incarnated spirit possessed by water spirit or even doing these works, worshiping the shrine/alusi mara ya etc. God is not Hippocratic. He will also not give you a gift that will go against his word. So look for your destiny.

The Work of a Native Doctor/Dibia

Native doctor is gift from God. Some people however misunderstand what a native doctor is. Anybody that has the gift of curing disease, who has knowledge of some roots and herbs and what they are used for, even in western way or African way are all gift from God.

The native doctor that is against the will of God, is the one that worships idols or shrines that sacrifices to other gods in the air, water, land, tree other than the sacrifice on the cross of Calvary. They are the ones that call on so many evil spirits those that do magic, the ones that invoke different evil spirits, and the ones that tie people, inye enyi ure, mbeafo, ntutu, or charms for protection and for progress. They are those for the devil.

But other native doctors that give native drugs, they are the main native doctors and do the same work with western doctors.

OMU (TENDER PALM FRONT)

The tender leaves of a palm tree (omu) are very potent in the Igbo cultural symbolography. The omu serves as a veritable tool of our social control by defining tones, bounds and actions. The omu is used to declare stop, exit, quit, in any location roped, tie, or put. When it is put on somebody's shop, it means that the owner of the shop is dead. When tied on any tree, it simply means that no one can pluck any fruit from that tree. When put on any compound, it means that somebody is dead there. If puts on an empty land, that show no trespass. Used to denote the degree of spirituality when held between the teeth.

PALM FRONT (IGU NKWU)

In Igbo land, palm front is symbolically used to show Peace and welcome. It is also the key factor that have radically altered the customs surrounding burials ceremony in Igbo culture (ima mkpukpu) And as part of the official mourning activities to commence "Ikwa ozu" celebrating the dead. A ceremony akin to a burial rites that allow the dead person to take their place among the ancestors.

CHAPTER 16

Destiny/Akara aka

Destiny is a gift from God given to all his creatures. According to Rev, Fr. Mario-David Dibie. (2003) "Destiny is what God want you to be" and it is not the same for example, it is not a must that everybody will be rich financially in this world. But people are after money as if to say there is no hope without it.

Different types of gift

There is one given the gift of money but not given that of sound thought or good health or peace, some have the gift of continent through fully blessing victory healing, knowing what the different plants can cure.

We have the gift of power to reveal secrets, power to go higher, teaching etc. Once you miss your destiny, it causes distress and backwardness to you. Next, it may be described as agwu or "Uchu". But mind you the greatest gift on earth is knowing and serving God.

If you are doing something but there is no progress like buying and selling or hand work, civil service etc. there are things you must look into. They are:

1. Is this/Are they your destiny?
2. Is there a curse?
3. Did you commit any curse or taboo?
4. Has the right time God destined for you come?

1. Are you at the right place?
2. Are you with something that is curse?
3. Will they give God glory?
4. Are you killing somebody, or siting on somebody's head?
5. Do you believe in God or human being or in your own power?

Other things you suppose to know
1. It is not a must that you will get everything you want as your wish.
2. Having them all does not mean that God loves you.
3. To be rich is not the only blessing from God.
4. Not having what you want, does not mean that God hate you.

Some of the men chosen by God as highly exalted are indeed very poor. They are seen as cursed. For example the family of Jesus Christ and other saints.

The Best Way to Seek For Our Destiny

There is no other way to locate our destiny if not to live a good life, to avoid sin, abomination, defiling the land, annoying God by not keeping His commandments. If you obey God, He will bring your destiny to light through prayers, your parents, your superiors and your efforts. If you look for your destiny in a different/another way, it will lead you to everlasting suffering because you have played into devil's hand that has come to kill and to destroy.

CHAPTER SEVENTEEN
Wines In Igbo land

There are three types of wine in Igbo land. They are 'Nkwu enu which some translate as 'Up wine', 'Ngwo' and ogwudu ana. 'Nkwu enu' or 'Up wine' is tapped from palm tree. The wine is tapped at the joint where the bunch of palm nut grows/Uduko/uzuke. The wine-tapper makes a hole at the place from which the wine drips into a calabash or plastic gallons provided for that purpose. The wine tapper is called 'Diochi' in Igbo land. The wine tapper has a lot of tools with which he taps his wine. These include rope for climbing the palm tree called (ETE), a pointed tool/Mmuma with which he makes his hole, a matchet or knife etc.

Good wine tapper

After the wine had been tapped, it is mixed with little water before it is sold in the market. If the wine tapper taps his wine without adding water, it is called 'Akulu-nkwu' grade one.

There are good and bad wine tappers. The wine from the good tapper is always good because he takes care to do his work by washing all the instruments with which he collects the wine from time to time adding to the fact that he does not add any other thing to the wine except a little water.

Bad Wine Tapper

A bad wine tapper is the one that plays with his job by not washing the instruments with which he taps his wine very well and regularly. He adds chemical substances like saccharine in his wine in order to make more money which has resulted in death to some consumers of up wine. He puts some leaves into his wine to make it sweeter adds a lot of water and also foreign wine to his wine etc. These culminate into sickness for those who are going to consume his wine. This is committing murder and also a taboo because it is tantamount to giving poison to people.

Ogwudu Ana Wine

This is a wine but not 'Nkwu enu' i.e. not 'up wine' it is always very sweet as if something is added to it but nothing is put in it. This type of wine is gotten from felled palm trees. To get this type of wine, the base of the palm is holed. Few days after making the hole, wine will start running from that hole. You can get up to two or three pots of wine from it in a day. Many people like and drink this wine but it is not good for the elders. Any person can tap this type of wine because it is easy but not everyone can tap the main wine which is 'Nkwu enu' because of the difficulty in tapping it. It doesn't run fast. The much it can give you in a day is half pot of wine or lesser.

Wine Intoxicated Palm Tree

There is a palm tree which God has created to produce only wine for the good of the people. These ones that produce wine do not produce palm nuts. Even when it produces palm nuts, the nuts are not good for use. If you cut the palm bunch, when it falls to the ground, it breaks. Another sign of knowing it is that you will always see bee swarming over its palm nut bunch. Some of them do not produce palm nut at all. Any good wine-tapper will be glad to have this type of palm tree because of its economic importance.

What is "Ngwo"

"Ngwo", a specie of palm wine is a tree God has given to people for production of wine called Raffia Palm. Some people call it "Ude" or "Ogoro". A good wine tapper looks for the one that is ready for tapping. When the tree is ripe for producing the wine. The tapper will now cut its frond, before it is tapped of wine. If the wine-tapper fails to cut this, this tree will start to produce "ude" nuts. This 'ude' nuts is used to produce necktie. It is also planted to produce another plant of the tree and eventually the tree itself. This tree flourishes most in a marshy area, in a clay soil/Abo-ude; sandy soil etc. there is also a type that is planted around the living house.

How 'Ngwo' is Tapped

'Ngwo' is not tapped as "Nkwu enu' is tapped. When the 'Ngwo' tree is ripe for tapping, the wine-tapper will cut the frond of that tree together with the supporting shelter that holds them. He then makes a hole at the base of that frond. After this, he will dress this opening some days before wine will start running from then. It can give more than one, two, three or four pots of wine in a day, and after some months, the tree is gone forever.

There is a specie of 'ngwo called "Okpannaa". This one germinates and stands alone whereas others can have up to three, four or five clusters etc. 'Okpanaa' tree produces profusely. It can give up to four or five pots of wine in a day. Starting from the day of tapping, the tree will last three weeks or more and die.

A Good "Ngwo" Wine-tapper

A good tapper of 'ngwo' takes good care of the wine he taps. He constantly changes or replaces all the leaves he used to covers his wine with because of bee, flies, sun heat and rainfall. He washes and cleans regularly his pot, calabashes or plastic gallons which he uses to collect the wine he sells to people. He doesn't ferment his wine with different leaves to make them sweeter for example or put another chemical for sweetening other than the required little water for those who want the one mixed with a little water. He knows that putting any other thing into the wine is a sin, a taboo and land defilement all of which can result in death. This is because it is murder since any other thing put inside the wine other than water can bring about death of some people since the body chemistry of everybody is not the same.

A Bad 'Ngwo' Wine-tapper

This type can use his wine to do everything possible just to make money that will destroy him. He ferments his wine by adding things like leaves, roots or stems of certain trees or grass just to make his wine to be sweet, taste like a good wine and be bigger, so that his money will be much. This has resulted in the death of many wine drinkers today, yet he claims that he has never killed any person, forgetting that he who poisons another person has committed abomination, whether the person you give it to dies or did not die.

How to serve Wine in A Public

When wine is brought in a public or gathering, it is the youngest man or male that serves the wine, the person to serve the wine will sit at the center of the gathering, first of all pour out one cup and drink by holding the pot of wine (calabash or gallon) with his left lap (thigh) and supports it with his left hand,. Anybody that drinks the win with his left hand is known as a bad person. The server will not shake the wine at the initial stage because the wine is still full. After drinking a cup, he gives a cup to the presenter of the wine after which he goes ahead to distribute the wine from his right hand or from the left side. In the case of a woman, who in turn receives it with both hands as mark of respect and honour. She must not drink it while standing or seated in the gathering with men; she squats down or sits somewhere before drinking half of the cup, and gives the half to her husband or nest to her husband as mark of respect. When the drink is finished, it is the people that will decide which elder should be given the bottom wine. It is left to this elder to give this last cup of wine to any person that has 'work at hand'. Having work at hand refers to newly married young man working to get a child or any man whose wife is still making babies. When this last cup is given out, the sharer of the wine will lie the pot flat to show any person coming in that the wine has finished in the pot. If the sharer does not tell the people that the wine has finished and drinks the bottom which contains the dregs of the pot or gives it to whoever that is not supposed, this brings misunderstanding to the extent that this person will buy another pot of wine in replacement and start to distribute it till he reaches the bottom and gives the last cup to the eldest to show the respect for the elders in Igbo society.

Wine For An Occasion

If an occasion is on, the ushers or servers will always be observant to know whatever each person came to the occasion with as gift. When a visitor carries anything to come, with cheerfulness, they will help him with that and with a joyful disposition welcome the person and receive the thing from him, and write the person's name on them for remembrance. These include pot, local baskets, plates or anything the person brings the gift with. They will also write his name in the book where they record what each person brought. If the person brings local wine, when the wine is brought down from his head, he the bringer will taste the wine to show that it is a drinkable substance before the server sends it inside to keep it at the barn or any conducive place.

If the donor of the wine does not taste it at this point, then when the wine is to be drunk, the sharer will first pour out a cup for him the donor, before he the sharer takes a cup before the public.

CHAPTER EIGHTEEN
Making a Will before One dies

Many a times before one dies, he indicates how his/her property should be shared. Those alive are bound to respect this will unless it is found to be against God's laws. At times, a son may have injured the father which may result in the father cheating the son in such a will. People may see such an action from the father as a bad one. At times because the person so favoured in a particular will and take care of the will maker when he/she was in sickness people who never knew what happened and may take it that the will was partially made against others. Because of this, before judging a particular will as good or bad, it is always advisable to know the circumstances that led to such arrangement, i.e. how things were when the will maker was alive that led him into dividing it the way he did. Not respecting the will of a dead person. This brings about evil to those who oppose the will.

INHERITING THE WEALTH OF A DEAD PERSON

If a dead person did not divide his/her belongings before death, those things will belong to those related to him/her people like his/her children, the husband or the wife, father or mother, his/her brothers/sisters or kindred or whoever sponsored his funeral service.

When somebody dies, if those people related to him i.e. those listed above decided not to bury the person, whoever sponsors his burial ceremony will inherit his belongings. (1965) No matter how related you are to the dead person, if you decide not to be involved in the running around and in the contribution no matter how small, when others finish the burial, eventually you come to share in the belongings of the dead, it is considered as defilement of the law which can kill.

What is funeral ceremony/ikwa ozu?

Funeral ceremony is one of the Igbo traditions that show that God created man in his own image and likeness. It is a way of showing human dignity and final respect to the dead person. It is always an agreement between the people about a share or due to be given to the deceased. Nnabuchi, Nwanwkwo (1987) Once it is agreed that when one of the group dies, such and such a thing should be done for the person and it has been happening for other people, if eventually a person dies and the people fail to give him/her his/her due because he or she cannot talk for himself or has no person to talk for him/her, it is a taboo which is going to be fought against by heavens or the earth. Unless this agreement have changed before this person dies.

CONSEQUENCES OF NOT BURYING A PERSON

Inability to give somebody burial can bring about curse and sudden death, sickness, lack of progress, barrenness, hardship etc. to the immediate family, or whoever that inherited his/her property. The one that fights for justice is God the upright judge. Once it is agreed that every dead person of the group should be buried, every dead is entitled to that, so that he/she goes in peace. Burial service is not worshiping idol, it is not idol sacrifice or placing untold burden upon the living. Burial is of two types. The good type and the evil type.

BURIAL WITH A GOOD TASTE: GOOD TYPE OF BURIAL

According to Igbo tradition, there is a laid-down procedure for breaking the news of death, especially that of a full-fledged man.

Informing the deceased's sons and daughter, mother's family should be a special event. The first group to be informed is the deceased's immediate family. Afterwards, the extended family are informed. Then the entire community and must be when the bereaved family deems it convenient.

When somebody dies, whoever is close to him mourns and is grieved that his/her person has passed on. He/she will tell others related to the person so that they know what happened. Maltreatment under the pretext of mourning or as evidence of innocence of the death of the deceased on the part of the surviving partner is all inhuman. Burial and funeral must be in accordance with the faith of the deceased person.

CORPSE OF A FULLFLEDGED MAN

When a man that has a family dies; his wife will inform his children and his closest brothers and sisters to know and come to see the man's corpse. The woman cannot carry the husband's corpse to the morgue or bury it without letting the people mentioned above to know that the person has died. Any woman that does this will not deny that she did kill the man when accused of that. It is the dead man's wife, sons, brothers or kindred that will decide how and where he is to be buried and how his funeral is to be performed. But the sons have upper hands in this if they are grown up.

Corpse of a Full Fledged Woman

If a woman dies, the husband will inform both her children and her brothers and sisters before she is deposited in the morgue or buried in the grave. If the man fails to do this and buries the wife by himself, this is a taboo and he will not be able to prove himself innocent of the woman's death when trouble comes. Igbos wash a corpse when somebody dies, dress her with one of her best clothes, it can be mother's clothe, fathers' clothe, a title clothe before he/she is put into a coffin and pray for her according to her faith before burying her. She is also given a befitting burial dance as well as re-acting whatever she was doing when she was alive, like one who used to make people laugh or who played a lot. If the death is not a sudden death or one considered not to have come at a certain ripe age, it is regarded as a celebration if the deceased family are rich. But if it is one considered to have come not at a ripe age, when he/she is buried, everybody will disperse. If one calls for celebration in such a burial, it is a misnomer and will not be encouraged. Igbos believes that long life is a blessing from God. If the person is of age and perhaps the family is up to the task, they can zill out drums to show that their father or mother lived a long life. This is acceptable. But while doing this, they should also realize that some of their neighbor have no food to eat, good house to live in, school fees, food, money to pay dues etc.

BURIAL WITH A BAD TASTE

Some people are using burial as a money making venture. Many a times, we see that burial in its actual sense is not what takes place; rather, people use this opportunity to rebuild their house, rebuilding their fence, repainting their houses and fence. The simple question is, why is it that this rebuilding and painting did not take place when the dead person was still alive. It is wrong to do this if you did not do it when the person was alive. Even when it is right to do it, and you can afford to rebuild a house and the fence within days, endeavour also to help those around you. Some use the burial ceremony as an opportunity to do evil and also make caricature of the dead person. While in some part of Igbo land, some use it to discriminate 'Amadi/Nwa-afo' son of the soil and Osu, This shows lack of serious thought. God created every human being in his image and likeness. Some use the opportunity to declare war on so many people and point accusing finger to a person they perceive as a killer of the dead person. Know that nothing is greater than God's power. As such, leave for God the giver of life, to look for what happened to the life he has given. Some others use burial as trading. When somebody comes for condolence, he will start inspecting what the person came with in order to know how to entertain the person. This shows that the person is not capable of the burial he has entered into. He who places a tray and expects to be given a bag of money should be ready to receive whatever is given to him by his sympathizers/visitors. Again, since the person shows that he wants to lavish money, he should also be prepared to give to whoever comes to him, what he demands, if you don't do it, pick and choose will come into your burial which would bring about criticism and animosity which will eventually arouse the resting spirits to rise and possibly attack you. Therefore, do your burial in accordance with your pocket.

SLAUGHTERING COW FOR SOMEBODY

Whoever wants to kill cow for his mother or father for burial celebrations should make inquiries before doing this. One is not supposed to do this when it was not done for his grandmother or grandfather. If not, this is a taboo in Igbo culture. It can be visited with a lot of consequences. It is already stated that the bone of an elder cuts like a knife. This is because your father is a child to the father that gave birth to him. As a result because you have not given your grandfather his dues, you cannot give to your father. You are not to give your father any due that is greater than that of his father. If you overlook this, be ready to accept whatever comes to you. However, whoever kills a cow for his father has joined the brand wagon of ogbu ehi.

Similarly, you cannot kill a cow for your mother if you have not done that for your father. If you do this, you are attracting to yourself problems you cannot handle. Very importantly, if you have not killed a cow for your father and mother, you cannot go for condolence to any other person with a cow. How can you slaughter cow to another person when you have not used cow to rest your father or mother in peace. It is a taboo in Igbo land. This is a respect to the elders.

It is some of these atrocities committed by Igbo sons and daughters that account for all the problems in Igbo land today.

Killing an Animal for burial/Ihe bu Akwamozu

The burial of a full-fledged man or woman in Igbo land is a law that the head of an animal with four legs should be cut, even if it is a small goat, if not it is an insult on the side of the deceased. Kill the goat and use the meat for entertainment. This slaughtering of animals must not have any performance of fetish rites, nor any part used or reserved for any ritual. After this custom whatever you are providing and cooking is as the size of your products. It might just be for entertainment of your visitors from a far place. In some town, no cooking of any kind you can use the meat for food for your kindred/Umunna, or family.

Concerning the death of a youth, both boys and girls, once he/she is buried the fellow youths will make some brief action before they disperse. The burial must be only one day.

The corpse of a child that is not up to 10 (ten) years is buried and the people will disperse. No ceremonies. Certain traditions like darting any corpse with a knife in the eye is not good, burying somebody with human heads, or putting something like knife, broom, hoe inside the coffin are all bad, things that can be done to arouse anger etc. are all bad. They are not supposed to be heard or talked about today in Igbo land.

Four market days in Igbo land

We have four markets days in Igbo land named; Eke, Orie, Afo, Nkwo. These four days make up one week in Igbo culture. These four markets are the days every town use to buy and sell food items etc. Awlaw town have Orie as their market, Ufuma which is located by the south have Afo as their market, Owere-ezukalla by the east have Eke, Inyi on the west have Nkwo while Achi on the north have eke as their market. No two nearby town will have the same market, because they are expected to join their neighbour on their market day. Every town does not perform their burial on their market days because everybody is expected to be in the market, but even if it must be on their market day, it is not a taboo. Saying that this person will not be buried this or that day simply because you call him, or her osu is a taboo. All men are equal in this case man or woman can be buried any day chosen by the family. For a man or woman of 50 years up, cannon gun shots/nkponala can be used for the burial ceremony to inform the town that funeral have begun etc.

CHAPTER NINETEEN
Knowing and touching the word of God

When everybody were doing things any how like many are doing today, God became angry and wanted to destroy all life, there was only one man by name, Noah whose family God used to establish the whole world. If you read the bible you will understand more than I am saying. (Gen. 6; 7) 'I will wipe out these people I have created, and also the animals and the birds, because I am sorry that I made any of them' There is no good or bad thing that you do in this life that is in vain, but it is patience that the Igbos don't have.

Not Having Patience

Not having patience is the curse that all the Igbos or ninety-nine percent of us have today together with unbelief but the sickness of not believing have reduced. Not exercising patience causes the Igbos not to wait on God, but everybody want their wish to be done not the will of God.

When one marries, within five years if the wife has not given birth, he will be restless and be moving aimlessly like the sheep that has broken from its tethers. If someone does business and has not made money over some years, he will be prepared to do anything to get the money which is ruling the world today. According to Fr. Eugene Ugonna Igboaja (1987) "You must also learn to wait, the fruit of your existential struggle may not be automatic" Believing in God that many people profess today is just on their lips. Anybody that falls sick for many years and has not gotten healing will start moving to many places to get healed and my question is this: All these things we do, and these places we go to who holds it and which spirit is in-charge? We all claim that the blessings of Abraham is for us but are we going to wait patiently for the number of years Abraham waited for his own blessings to manifest? May you use your tongue to count your teeth.

CHAPTER TWENTY

Advice to the youth

Every youth should know that life is war; the way you are is the way you live. Where a tree faces is where it will fall, the world is once you eat, you give to the other. You will be like what you worship. The cup you are using for measurement they will use for you. So after being a youth, you will also become old. All these mean early to bed early to rise. So build your life accordingly on time for you to receive good thing. Don't say that they all doing this and they do that which means you will do same, 'no'. The question is this; will you endure like them once the time reaches? You will die like them when it is time also?. Everything you do on earth, you shall receive the judgment. Education is good, because it helps you to know your left and right, it will also help you to have wisdom, and also to know the right thing and do it at the right time.

Do not follow any bad group or persons; do no worship another god except your God which is in heaven, your maker. Through the direction in this book or the word of God or the other good books of the tings through Christ Jesus. He that have ear let him hear.

Advice to the Church

Everybody that goes to church should know that church is not by word of mouth but character. Going around with Bible, wearing turtle neck cloths, preaching the gospel every morning, covering your ear with hair tie, sleeping in the church daily etc. All this are good but Going to church, what it means is that you have belief in the teachings of our Lord Jesus Christ, it means that the person will be ready to surrender his/her life or the life of your wife, husband, children, mother, father at all time because of your faith in (CHRIST JESUS). A person like this does not use condition like: husband, or wife, money, sickness, joblessness, hunger, life or death etc. as reasons to lose hope in Christ. You should know all these so that going to church will not be in vain at last or become a disgrace to you. Anybody that believes in Christ has nothing to do with the world again or thinking about what the devil/world will do to him because they have no power over you. Belief in Christ means that you stand firm and so know what they teach you about Christ. If you are having double mind in Christ, you don't need to call yourself a child of God.

The leaders of the church should know that they are not called to eat the children of God but to teach and direct them in rightful ways of God. There are some language we speak, 'Ndi na-ago mmuo' the 'spirit worshippers'. This is not supposed to be. Instead, the idol worshippers/ndiogo arusi. But in Igbo land, some are Christians while some are idol worshippers others join the secret society etc. So we should use our language very well and not to use it to criticize the church.

People of Igbo, we should stop deceiving ourselves by stepping one foot in church, while the other is in the shrine or other secret society, remember that you should bear the consequences at last. There is every tendency for those that want to worship the devil, in the other hand, if you want to worship God you are free. But if you believe in Christ you will be free from sin, and other evil thing that Christ condemned, without doing all these you are deceiving yourself and remember that after death judgment follows.

Those that believe in Devil

If you believe in devil and you also work for him, remember that you will have a reward. Those that worship idol/alusi, secret society, marine kingdom, witches and wizards, occult men and women, blood suckers, evil planters etc. continue doing the ones you belong to it and be bold, so that at last you will receive a great reward, don't worry it is better you are fully devoted on the one you are doing than that you are hidden. But if I may advice you, I will tell you to serve the living God, your Creator for He is the alpha and omega and He alone have the final word. Remember at the end, you will have the reward of good or bad work. For they say a stitch in time saves nine.

PRAYER FOR IGBO RACE;

God our heavenly father, we thank you (3 times). Oh God you are the creator and the originator of the Igbo race your people. Right now, we are deeply sorry in our heart for the many atrocities, taboos, sins and worshiping of false gods (idols) instead of you the creator. Please have mercy on us and may your hot and terrible anger on us be calmed down. Do not destroy us as we deserved, but support us with your grace and mercy for which you are known. You alone know the best way of gathering us your children together and making us one. Nobody, no god (spirit), nor anything else can save us, if you do not save us. Please have mercy on us all. We, the entire Igbo race call upon you with one voice to come down in power and glory. Come and destroy the person, god or anything that is bringing about division, scattering of our people and unbelief between yourself and ourselves, so that with happy hearts we will live and worship you in the land that you gave to us, please put new spirit in us, so that we will have love for one another in order to speak and act always with one mind. We ask you this through Jesus Christ our Lord, Amen.

EKPERE MAKA UMU IGBO

Chineke nna anyi. Anyi na-ekele gi(3 times).Chineke, obu gi kere anyi bu umu Igbo ka anyi buru ndi nke gi. Ona-ewute anyi n'obi ugbua n'ihi oke aru, nso, njo, na ihapu ife so Gi bu Chi okike na-efe ihe I kere eke. Biko meere anyi ebere ka iwe gi dioku dajuo. E bibina anyi dika anyi si kwesi, ma were obiebere ejirimara Gi kwagide anyi. O bu so gi mara uzo kacha nma iji kpokoba anyi bu umu gi onu ma mee ka anyi buru otu. Odighi onye, chi, mobu ihe puru inaputa anyi na-abughi Gi. Biko mere anyi ebere. Anyi bu umu Igbo niile ji otu olu n'akpo gi ka I gbadata na ike na ebube. Bia bibie onye, chi, mobu ihe n'ebute nkewa, kposaa, ekwekwe na etiti anyi na Gi, kanyi wee were obi anuri biri ma n'efekwa Gi n'ala inyere anyi. Biko tinye mmuo ohuu nime anyi kanyi wee hukorita onweanyi n'anya wee nwee ike ikwu ofu mee ofu. Anyi yoro nkea n'aha Jesu onye nzoputanyi amen isee.

BIBLIOGRAPHY

(1) M. C. M. IDIGO (1955) Aguleri history and culture. Bantam press limited 18, Okeho Street, Ireakari Estate, Isolo-Lagos.
(2) Victor M. C. Eyisi (2010) Igbo History. Chuvic Int'L Agency Ltd no. 5 Okwuenu Street Fegge, Onisha.
(3) Genesis. 11; 10, 26. Good News Bible Today's English Version.
(4) Chisom Ani (2004)complete information on Baifra.
(5) C. V. C. Okekenta (2012) Emmarox Press 44, McDermott Road, Warri.
(6) Norwich (1994) the interesting narrative of the life of Mr. Olaudah Equiano.
(7) Uche P. Ikeanyibe Pro ft. The quest for the origin of the Igbo people, Maadadona P and P House, Lagose (2005)
(8) Eric C. N. Okam (2004) the Igbos as descendants of Jacob, Snaap Press Ltd Enugu.
(9) Atodo P.A and Obiorah C.C (2012) Nigerian government and politics Scoa Heritage systems no 8 Onwurah street Awka.
(10) Directives on burial funeral ceremonies in Awgu Diocese, Snaap Press Ltd, 1 Snaap Drive, Independence Layout Enugu.
(11) Journal Bigard Memorial Seminary Enugu. Vol,25 no 1.Jan-June,2005.
(12) Rev. Fr. Ezebuchi Paschalis Agu(1996) Born to Love. Fabson Graphics 233 Agbani road/1 Kenneth rd. Awkunanaw Enugu.
(13) Rev. R.J. Griffin Where is the truth. St. Anthony's bookshop 15, old Ojo road Agboju Amuwo, Lagos.
(14) Chikwelu A. Emmanuel (2008) The people for Africa's rebirth, page5.Tsporm publishing (Nig) no. 20 Ndizuogu rd. Akokwa.
(15) Rev. Fr. Ezebuchi P. Agu (2004) secret of success in marriage. Ifeson prints, 2 Neni str. Ogui New layout Enugu.
(16) Rev. Fr. Joseph Nwilo (2003) Formation of a child's personality, Rex Charles and Patricks Ltd. Nimo
(17) Chukwuemeka Nweke. Infidelity in marriage. Mid-Field publishers Ltd, 28 Okosi rd. Onisha.
(18) Ajakemo, B.C. and Aroh, E.C. (2003) Public service system in Nigeria. 159 Upper Chime, New Haven, Enugu.
(19) Pita Ejiofor (2006)ibeku ndi-Igbo maka asusu Igbo. Nolix educational publishcation (Nig) 35 Amawbia sreet, Uwani Enugu.

(20) Rev. Fr. Eugene U. Igboaja. (1987) time on my hand, Lay Apostolate publication Enugu. printed by Snaap press 46 Udoji Enugu.
(21) Rev. Fr.Dr. Innocent Ekumauche Okoh (1994) to love and to cherish. Mbeyi and associates (Nig) Ltd. 23, Mukandasi Street, Okota, Isolo, Lagos.
(22) Wheaton, Illinois (1974) for women only. Faith builder publication 339, Aba.
(23) Wheaton, Illinois (1973) for men only. Faith builder publication 339, Aba.
(24) Encyclopedia of Biblical Interpretation, by Menahem M. Kasher, Vol. II, 1955, p.79.
(25) Jewish Antiquities, I, 114,115 (IV, 2, 3).
(26) Things Fall Apart by Chinua Achebe.
(27) F. Chidozie Ogbalu & E Nolue Emenanjo.
(28) Onwuejeogwu, (1975).
(29) Isichei.
(30) Elizabeth Allo (1997)
(31) A History of African Societies to (1870).
(32) Hammer, Jill. (2006)Cambridge University Press. The Jewish book ofdays: a companion for all seasons. Jewish Publication Society.p. 224. ISBN 0-8276-0831-4
(33) Olaudah Equiano, the Interesting Narrative of the Life of Olaudah Equiano, or Gustavus Vassa, the Africa.
(34) Chikwelu Anietoo-chukwu E. (2008).
(35) Editorial of Bigard Theological Studies (2005).
(36) Daughters of St. Paul (1994).
(37) Englewoods Cliffs (1966). Isichei, Elizabeth (1978). Igbo Worlds. Institute for the Study of Human Issues.
(38) Slattery, Katharine. "The Igbo People - Origins & History". Www.faculty.ucr.edu. School of English, Queen's University of Belfast. Retrieved April 20, 2016.
(39) Chigere, Nkem Hyginus (20002. Chigere, Nkem Hyginus (2000). Foreign Missionary Background and Indigenous Evangelization in Igboland: Igboland and The Igbo People of Nigeria. Transaction Publishers, USA. p. 17. ISBN 3-8258-4964-3. Retrieved January 17, 2016.
(40)Williams, Lizzie (2008). 1. Ogbaa, Kalu (1999). "Cultural Harmony I: Igboland – the World of Man and the World of Spirits".

Understanding Things Fall Apart. Greenwood Publishing. p. 106. ISBN 0-313-30294-4. Bradt Travel Guides. p. 32. ISBN 1-84162-239-7.
(41) Ogbaa, Kalu (1999). "Cultural Harmony I: Igboland – the World of Man and the World of Spirits". Understanding Things Fall Apart. Greenwood Publishing. p. 106. ISBN 0-313-30294-4.
(42) Ogbaa, Kalu (1999). "Cultural Harmony I: Igboland – the World of Man and the World of Spirits". Understanding Things Fall Apart. Greenwood Publishing. p. 106. ISBN 0-313-30294-4.
(43) Forsythe, Frederick (2006). Shadows: Airlift and Airwar in Biafra and Nigeria 1967–1970. p. 1. ISBN 1-902109-63-5.
(44) Adekson, Adedayo Oluwakayode (2004). The "civil society" problematique: deconstructing civility and southern Nigeria's ethnic radicalization. Routledge. pp. 87, 96. ISBN 0-415-94785-5.
(45) Mwakikagile, Godfrey (2006). 2. Mwakikagile, Godfrey (2006). African Countries: An Introduction with Maps. Pan-African Books: Continental Press. p. 86. ISBN 0-620-34815-1.
(46) Levinson, David; Timothy J O'Leary (1995). Encyclopedia of World Cultures. G.K. Hall. p. 120. ISBN 0-8161-1815-9.
(47) Levinson, David; Timothy J O'Leary (1995). Encyclopedia of World Cultures. G.K. Hall. p. 120. ISBN 0-8161-1815-9.
(48) "Ibo" in the Encyclopædia Britannica, 11th ed. 1911.
(49) Lovejoy, Paul (20002. Lovejoy, Paul (2000). Identity in the Shadow of Slavery. Continuum International Publishing Group. p. 58. ISBN 0-8264-4725-2.
(50) Floyd, E. Randall (2002). 2. Floyd, E. Randall (2002). In the Realm of Ghosts and Hauntings. Harbor House. p. 51. ISBN 1-891799-06-1.
(51) Cassidy, Frederic Gomes; Robert Brock Le Page (2002). A Dictionary of Jamaican English (2nd ed.). University of the West Indies Press. p. 168. ISBN 976-640-127-6.
(52) Equiano, Olaudah (1837). The Interesting Narrative of the Life of Olaudah Equiano. I. Knapp. p. 27.
(53) Obichere, Boniface I. (1982). Studies in Southern Nigerian History: A Festschrift for Joseph Christopher Okwudili Anene 1918–68. Routledge. p. 207. ISBN 0-7146-3106-X.
(54) Elizabeth, Isichei (1976). A History of the Igbo People. London: Macmillan. ISBN 0-333-18556-0.; excerpted in "Cultural Harmony I: Igboland — the World of Man and the World of Spirits",

section 4 of Kalu Ogbaa, ed., Understanding Things Fall Apart (Westport, Conn.: Greenwood Press, 1999; ISBN 0-313-30294-4), pp. 83–85.
(55) Apley, Apley. "Igbo-Ukwu (ca. 9th century)". The Metropolitan Museum of Art. Retrieved 2008-11-23.
(56) Isichei, Elizabeth Allo (1997). A History of African Societies to 1870. Cambridge University Press Cambridge, UK. p. 512. ISBN 0-521-45599-5.
(57) Lovejoy, Paul (2000). Identity in the Shadow of Slavery. Continuum International Publishing Group. p. 62. ISBN 0-8264-4725-2.
(58) Chambers, Douglas B. (2005). Murder at Montpelier: Igbo Africans in Virginia (illustrated Ed.). Univ. Press of Mississippi. p. 33. ISBN 1-57806-706-5.
(59) Basden, George Thomas (1921). Among the Ibos of Nigeria: An Account of the Curious & Interesting Habits, Customs & Beliefs of a Little Known African People, by One who Has for Many Years Lived Amongst Them on Close & Intimate Terms. Seeley, Service. p. 184.
(70) Hodder, Ian (1987). The Archaeology of Contextual Meanings (illustrated ed.). CUP Archive. p. 72. ISBN 0-521-32924-8.
(71) Hodder, Ian (1987). The Archaeology of Contextual Meanings (illustrated ed.). CUP Archive. p. 72. ISBN 0-521-32924-8.
(72) Furniss, Graham; Elizabeth Gunner; Liz Gunner (1995). Power, Marginality and African Oral Literature. Cambridge University Press. p. 65. ISBN 0-521-48061-2.
(73) Chigere, Nkem Hyginus M. V. (2001). Foreign Missionary Background and Indigenous Evangelization in Igboland (illustrated ed.). LIT Verlag Berlin-Hamburg-Münster. p. 113. ISBN 3-8258-4964-3.
(73) Ilogu, Edmund (1974). Christianity and Ibo culture. Brill Archive. p. 11. ISBN 90-04-04021-8.
(74) Ndukaihe, Vernantius Emeka; Fonk, Peter (2006). Achievement as Value in the Igbo/African Identity: The Ethics. LIT Verlag Berlin-Hamburg-Münster. p. 204. ISBN 3-8258-9929-2.
(75) Agbasiere, Joseph Thérèse (2000). Women in Igbo Life and Thought. Routledge. p. 12. ISBN 0-415-22703-8. Retrieved 2008-12-19.
(76) Chambers, Douglas B. (2005). Murder at Montpelier: Igbo

Africans in Virginia (illustrated ed.). Univ. Press of Mississippi. p. 183. ISBN 1-57806-706-5.
(77) Liamputtong, Pranee (2007). Childrearing and Infant Care Issues: A Cross-cultural Perspective. Nova Publishers. p. 155. ISBN 1-60021-610-2.
(78) Holbrook, Jarita C.; R. Thebe Medupe; Johnson O. Urama. African Cultural Astronomy: Current Archaeoastronomy and Ethnoastronomy Research in Africa. Springer, 2007. p. 235. ISBN 1-4020-6638-4.
(79) Holbrook, Jarita C. (2007). African Cultural Astronomy: Current Archaeoastronomy and Ethnoastronomy Research in Africa.
Springer. p. 35. ISBN 1-4020-6638-4. Retrieved 2008-01-10.
(80) Njoku, Onwuka N. (2002). Pre-colonial economic history of Nigeria. Ethiope Publishing Corporation, Benin City, Nigeria. ISBN 978-2979-36-8.
(81) Onwuejeogwu, M. Angulu (1981). An Igbo civilization: Nri kingdom & hegemony. Ethnographica. ISBN 978-123-105-X.
(82) Aguwa, Jude C. U. (1995). The Agwu deity in Igbo religion. Fourth Dimension Publishing Co., Ltd. p. 29. ISBN 978-156-399-0.
(83) Hammer, Jill (2006). The Jewish book of days: a companion for all seasons. Jewish Publication Society. p. 224. ISBN 0-8276-0831-4.
(84) Peek, Philip M.; Kwesi Yankah (2004). African Folklore: An Encyclopedia (illustrated ed.). Taylor & Francis. p. 299. ISBN 0-415-93933-X.
(85) Shillington, Kevin (2005). Encyclopedia of African History. CRC Press. p. 674. ISBN 1-57958-245-1.
(86) Uchendu, Victor Chikezie (1965). The Igbo of southeast Nigeria (illustrated ed.). Holt, Rinehart and Winston. p. 4. ISBN 0-03-052475-X.
(87) Glenny, Misha (2008). Mc Mafia Seriously Organised Crime. Random House. p. 200. ISBN 0-09-948125-1.
(88) Williams, Emily Allen (2004). The Critical Response to Kamau Brathwaite. Praeger Publishers. p. 235. ISBN 0-275-97957-1.
(89) "Edward Wilmot Blyden". Microsoft Encarta Online Encyclopedia. Archived from the original on 31 October 2009. Retrieved 19 November 2008.
(90) "Edward Wilmot Blyden:- Father of Pan Africanism (August 3, 1832 to February 7, 1912)". Awareness Times (Sierra Leone). 2 August 2006.

(91) Robeson II, Paul (2001). The Undiscovered Paul Robeson: An Artist's Journey, 1898–1939 (PDF). Wiley. p. 3. ISBN 0-471-24265-9. Retrieved 2008-12-27. A dark-skinned man descended from the Ibo tribe of Nigeria, Reverend Robeson was of medium height with broad shoulders, and had an air of surpassing dignity.
(92) Azuonye, Chukwuma (1990). "Igbo Names in the Nominal Roll of Amelié, An Early 19th Century Slave Ship from Martinique: Reconstructions, Interpretations and Inferences". footnote: University of Massachusetts Boston. p. 1. Retrieved 2015-03-26.
(93) Guo, Rongxing (2006). Territorial Disputes and Resource Management: A Global Handbook. Nova Publishers. p. 130. ISBN 1-60021-445-2.
(94) Bight of Biafra. Britannica Online Encyclopedia. Retrieved 2008-11-19.
(95) Chambers, D.B. "REJOINDER – The Significance of Igbo in the Bight of Biafra Slave". Routledge, part of the Taylor & Francis Group. Retrieved 2009 01 23.
(96) Bonny. Britannica Online Encyclopedia. Retrieved 2008-12-27.
(97) Douglas, Chambers B. (2005). Murder at Montpelier: Igbo Africans in Virginia. Univ. Press of Mississippi. p. 25. ISBN 1-57806-706-5.
(98) Talbot, Percy Amaury; Mulhall, H. (1962). The physical anthropology of Southern Nigeria. Cambridge University Press. p. 5.
(99) Lovejoy, Paul E. (2003). Trans-Atlantic Dimensions of Ethnicity in the African Diaspora. Continuum International Publishing Group. pp. 92–93. ISBN 0-8264-4907-7.
(100) Isichei, Elizabeth Allo (2002). Voices of the Poor in Africa. Boydell & Brewer. p. 81.
(101) Rucker, Walter C. (2006). The River Flows on: Black Resistance, Culture, and Identity Formation in Early America. LSU Press. p. 52. ISBN 0-8071-3109-1.
(102) Holloway, Joseph E. (2005). Africanisms in American Culture. bottom of 3rd paragraph: Indiana University Press. p. 32. ISBN 0-253-21749-0. Retrieved 2008-12-19.
(103) Philips, John Edward (2005). Writing African History. Boydell & Brewer. p. 412. ISBN 1-58046-164-6.
(104) Berlin, Ira. "African Immigration to Colonial America". History Now. (paragraph 11) Preferences on both side of the Atlantic determined, to a considerable degree, which enslaved Africans went

where and when, populating the mainland with unique combinations of African peoples and creating distinctive regional variations in the Americas.

(105) Morgan, Philip D.; Sean Hawkins (2004). Black Experience and the Empire. Oxford University Press. p. 82. ISBN 0-19-926029-X.

(106) "Ethnic Identity in the Diaspora and the Nigerian Hinterland". Toronto, Canada: York university. Retrieved 2008-11-23. As is now widely known, enslaved Africans were often concentrated in specific places in the diaspora...USA (Igbo)

(107) Appiah, Anthony; Henry Louis Gates. Africana. p. 212. ISBN 0-465-00071-1.

(108) Craton, Michael. Roots and Branches. University of Waterloo Dept. of History. p. 125. ISBN 0-08-025367-9.

(109) McWhorter, John H. (2005). Defining Creole. Oxford University Press US. p. 217. ISBN 0-19-516670-1. Retrieved 2009-01-10.

(110) Robotham, Don (January 13, 2008). "Jamaica and Africa (Part II)". Gleaner Company. Retrieved 2008-11-23. ...It is not possible to declare that the Eastern Nigerian influence in Jamaica – apparent in expressions such as 'red ibo' – is Igbo.

(111) Allsopp, Richard; Jeannette Allsopp (2003). Dictionary of Caribbean English Usage. Contributor Richard Allsopp. University of the West Indies Press. p. 101. ISBN 976-640-145-4.

(112) Carrington, Sean (2007). A~Z of Barbados Heritage. Macmillan Caribbean Publishers Limited. p. 25. ISBN 0-333-92068-6.

(113) Gibbs, Archibald Robertson (1883). British Honduras: an historical and descriptive account of the colony from its settlement, 1670. S. Low, Marston, Searle & Rivington. Eboe Town, a section of the town of Belize reserved for that African tribe, was destroyed by fire

(114) Fischer, David Hackett; Kelly, James C. (2000). Bound Away: Virginia and the Westward Movement. University of Virginia Press. p. 62. ISBN 0-8139-1774-3.

(115) Opie, Frederick Douglass (2008). Hog and Hominy: Soul Food from Africa to America. Columbia University Press. p. 18. ISBN 0-231-14638-8.

(116) vington. Eboe Town, a section of the town of Belize reserved for that African tribe, was destroyed by fire

(117) "list of languages #25 along with Kru and Yoruba" (PDF). U.S. ENGLISH Foundation, Inc. Retrieved 2009-01-10.
(118) Ekechi, Felix K. (1972). Missionary Enterprise and Rivalry in Igboland, 1857–1914 (illustrated ed.). last paragraph on page 146: by Routledge. p. 146. ISBN 0-7146-2778-X.
(119) Chuku, Gloria (2005). Igbo Women and Economic Transformation in Southeastern Nigeria, 1900–1960: 1900–1960 (illustrated ed.). Routledge. p. 145. ISBN 0-415-97210-8.
(120) Afigbo, A. E. (1992). Groundwork of Igbo history. Lagos: Vista Books. pp. 522–541. ISBN 978-134-400-8.
(121) Furniss, Graham; Elizabeth Gunner; Liz Gunner (1995). Power, Marginality and African Oral Literature. Cambridge University Press. p. 67. ISBN 0-521-48061-2.
(122) Ilogu, Edmund (1974). Christianity and Ibo Culture. Brill Archive. p. 63. ISBN 90-04-04021-8.
(123) Sanday, Peggy Reeves (1981). Female Power and Male Dominance: On the Origins of Sexual Inequality (illustrated, reprint ed.). Cambridge University Press. p. 136. ISBN 0-521-28075-3.
(124) Gordon, April A. (2003). Nigeria's Diverse Peoples. ABC-CLIO. p. 87. ISBN 1-57607-682-2. Retrieved 2008-12-19.
(125) Rubin, Neville. Annual Survey of African Law. Routledge, 1970. p. 20. ISBN 0-7146-2601-5.
(126) Fielding, Steven; John W. Young (2003). The Labour Governments 1964–1970: International Policy. Manchester University Press. p. 197. ISBN 0-7190-4365-4.
(127) Mathews, Martin P. (2002). Nigeria: Current Issues and Historical Background. Nova Publishers. p. 38. ISBN 1-59033-316-0.
(128) Minogue, Martin; Judith Molloy (1974). African Aims & Attitudes: Selected Documents. General C. O. Ojukwu: CUP Archive. p. 393. ISBN 0-521-20426-7.
(129) Bocquené, Henri; Oumarou Ndoudi; Gordeen Gorder (2002). Memoirs of a Mbororo: The Life of Ndudi Umaru, Fulani Nomad of Cameroon. Berghahn Books. p. 285. ISBN 1-57181-844-8.
(130) Diamond, Stanley (June 1967). "The Biafra Secession". Africa Today. Indiana University Press. **14** (3): 1–2. doi:10.2307/4184781 (inactive 2015-01-09). JSTOR 4184781.
(131) Keil, Charles (January 1970). "The Price of Nigerian Victory". Africa Today. Indiana University Press. **17** (1). JSTOR 4185054.
(132) "John Lennon". Rock and Roll Hall of Fame + Museum. 2007.

Retrieved 2008-11-24. September 1, 1969: John Lennon returns his MBE. He says it is to protest the British government's involvement in Biafra, its support of the U.S. in Vietnam and the poor chart performance of his latest single, 'Cold Turkey'.

(133) "Call for Biafra to leave Nigeria". BBC. 6 July 2007. Retrieved 2008-11-23.

(134) Howard-Hassmann, Rhoda E. (1986). Human Rights in Commonwealth Africa. Rowman & Littlefield. p. 95. ISBN 0-8476-7433-9. Retrieved 2008-12-18.

ABOUT THE AUTHOR

Mr. Ugochukwu Benjamin Ikeokwu is the writer of this book. He was a student of Federal Polytechnic Oko where he did his course in Public Administration.

Ugochukwu Benjamin Ikeokwu has a strong call in Igbo land which led him out of seminary to answer the call from God for the sake of Igbo nation. He is the founder of Bijec International and also a correspondent of **"KPAKPANDO TV WORLD WIDE"** and executive member Otu Suwakwa Igbo(Nigeria) INITIATIVE'. Former P.G Isiama Awlaw Autonomous community. He is the CEO **"BIJEC movies INTERNATIONAL"** A native of Umuaro Umukabia Isiama Awlaw in Oji River Local Government of Enugu State.

1. **Our company**, BIJEC MOVIES INTERNATIONAL is a private registered company in Nigeria on the issues of Music/film production, General merchandise/trading, General contracts. BIJEC is borne out of a desire for the promotion of Igbo language and culture. BIJEC MOVIES INTERNATIONAL have been in the forefront of campaign of uniting the Igbos and a channel designed to clean up the hard slap of the Western culture and traditions on our faces. We are also the major representative of Igbos in the issues that concern culture and traditions of our people. We have always done our nation proud. BIJEC Enterprise was among the first listed contingents that represented Anambra State in the 7th African Arts and crafts, Expo 2014, at the Eagle square Abuja. 27 countries participated including China and Korea. All the 36 state of Nigeria also participated. I am delighted to in- form you here that we won three positions. In 2014, BIJEC won the 2nd Igbo film cup competition presented by Chief Godwin Ezeemo to Otu-SuwakwaIgbo Nigeria Initiative.

BIJEC have received many award from Ohaneze ndi-Igbo, Igbo film forum/Ohaneze/Nollywood etc. We have over two hundred and fifty members throughout Igbo land, and you are free to join with the promoting spirit of oneness among Igbo, not minding state of Origin.

2. **PRAYER FOR IGBO RACE;** God our heavenly father, we thank you (3 times). Oh God you are the creator and the originator of the Igbo race your people. Right now, we are deeply sorry in our heart for the many atrocities, taboos, sins and worshiping of false gods (idols) instead of you the creator. Please have mercy on us and may your hot and terrible anger on us be calmed down. Do not destroy us as we deserved, but support us with your grace and mercy for which you are known. You alone knows the best way of gathering us your children together and making us one. Nobody, no god (spirit), nor anything else can save us, if you do not save us. Please have mercy on us all. We, the entire Igbo race call upon you with one voice to come down in power and glory. Come and destroy the person, god or anything that is bringing about division, scattering of our people and unbelief between yourself and ourselves, so that with happy hearts we will live and worship you in the land that you gave to us, please put new spirit in us, so that we will have love for one another in order to speak and act always with one mind. We ask you this through Jesus Christ our Lord, Amen.

Printed in Poland
by Amazon Fulfillment
Poland Sp. z o.o., Wrocław